Praise

"*Bliss Road* is a raw and real memoir, illuminating the complicated path of a neurodiverse family fixed in a legacy between trepidation and tenderness; a legacy that may well have repeated itself had it not been for Engber's ability to face the mirror and find the answers to the questions she didn't even know she had about autism and the power of love."
LIANE HOLLIDAY WILLEY, AUTHOR OF *PRETENDING TO BE NORMAL: LIVING WITH ASPERGERS SYNDROME*

"With bracing honesty, and rare insight, Martha Engber's courageous, highly readable account of her experience as the child of a parent with undiagnosed ASD is compelling, joyous and inspiring.'"
BYDDI LEE, AUTHOR OF *THE REJUVENATION TRILOGY*

"In *Bliss Road*, Martha Engber takes the reader on a candid and poetic journey through her life with a neuroatypical father. A glorious blend of insights and wisdom, this memoir may just be what we need to deepen our human capacity for love and understanding."
IMI LO, AUTHOR OF *EMOTIONAL SENSITIVITY AND INTENSITY: HOW TO MANAGE INTENSE EMOTIONS AS A HIGHLY SENSITIVE PERSON*

About the Author

Martha Engber is the author of *Winter Light*, an IPPY Gold Medal Winner in Young Adult Fiction. Her other books include the novels *The Falcon, The Wolf and the Hummingbird*, and *The Wind Thief*; and the resource for writers, *Growing Great Characters from the Ground Up*. A speaker and work-shop facilitator, she's had dozens of short stories and poems published in literary magazines and a play produced in Hollywood. She lives in California with her husband, bike and surfboard. She invites readers to connect via her website, *MarthaEngber.com*.

MARTHA ENGBER

BLISS ROAD

a memoir about living a lie and coming to terms with the truth

V

www.vineleavespress.com

To my sisters, my heroes

Author's Note

I'm the first to admit memory is fallible, which is not so much an opinion as it is a fact based on conclusive scientific studies. All I, or anyone, can be sure of regarding our pasts are the feelings we're left with, those ghostly remnants that haunt the attic of our lives. Where possible I've corroborated memories and dates via journal entries and conversations with those involved. In others, I rely on those spectral internal spirits and my robust imagination to recreate the dialogue and settings that led to significant, verifiable moments. I'm forever in debt to everyone who has been part of my journey—even the potholed segments—and especially to those in my family for their love and support.

Part I
Dad

Bliss Road

There is a sign, *Bliss
Road*,

naming a narrow
lane

atop a high New
England hill

the letters, writ
in white,

radiant in the
glow

of a dusk
summer

sun, the view
beyond

the sign a seeming
forever

of tender green
hills

rolling easy
around

the blue
cool

of a calm
lake.

To cross the
line,

to reach the
other

place takes but
a few

steps across
an uneven

width of
black

pavement in
heavy

neck-breaking
shadow.

I was forty-one when my mom told me a disturbing story about my dad.

An early August evening, we were sitting on her deck with a glass of wine in hand. As we talked, I gazed at her beautiful backyard that featured a tree topped by a massive head of burgundy-colored leaves. Flowers and blooming shrubs bordering the expanse of lush lawn offered bursts of crimson, yellow and white. Occasionally, Mom pointed out changes she intended to make.

"That rhododendron isn't doing well back there. Too much shade. I'm going to put it up front where it can flourish, by that bush closest to the neighbors' driveway. You know where I'm talking about?"

Some years previous, she and Dad had moved from New Jersey to this small Connecticut town to be near Deanna and Sue, my two older sisters and their families. Every summer I flew out to visit for two weeks. When my sisters and I began having kids, those vacations overflowed with morning coffee and bagels on the deck, long beach days on Long Island Sound, and noisy barbecues on humid evenings.

Though our kids eventually grew up and moved on, I continued the summer sojourn, during which the days maintained a familiar flow. My sisters, Mom and I would spend the morning and afternoon on an adventure, because Mom loved nothing better than to *go and do*. We'd bike a paved path through a forest of tall oaks or wander picturesque seaside towns, the sky noisy with seagulls. We walked amid the reverential silence of art museums, our footsteps echoing. We'd float on our backs in the ocean while staring up at the pink of a sunsetting sky.

On our way to and from our destinations, we listened to Mom's favorite music. As the likes of Helen Reddy, Doris Day and Frank Sinatra sang, she'd rhapsodize about the beauty of our surrounds, whether a sunset, ocean or meadow.

Spectacular!

Just gorgeous!

Have you ever seen anything like it? It's just ... glorious!

Adventure complete, my sisters would return to their homes and families to clean up, whereas I'd stay with my parents. After showering, my mom and I would sit on her deck, as we did on this particular evening. Music drifted through the screen door of her and Dad's little ranch house. Her freckled legs stretched out before her, ankles crossed, she sipped the cheap wine she'd grown to love during her years of economizing during the inflationary 1970s. Rosy, bubbly, and light on actual alcohol, the wine matched her outlook on life and memories. She often told us stories of growing up in her small upstate New York town where she, two of her three sisters and other friends would roam the forests and swim in lakes and rivers.

We had so much fun, she'd say, smiling and shaking her head.

She rarely recalled anything unpleasant and never talked negatively about Dad, a mostly gentle, conscientious man who loved her dearly. Instead, she reminded my sisters and me that all fathers had oddities. Dee, Sue and I assumed that must be true because we didn't have another dad with whom to compare him. We felt lucky he was ninety-five percent kind and loving.

It was that last five percent that made Dad unusual in an inexplicable way. He didn't have mental health problems or addictions to drugs or alcohol. Though he'd been in the Army during the end of the Korean War, he hadn't seen any action, so the chance seemed low that he suffered from Post-Traumatic Stress Disorder. Fortunately, he hadn't been abused as a child, but instead had been the oldest of five kids in a working-class Catholic family in Alton, IL.

Yet, occasionally, Mom would let her doubt about him slip, that sometimes his decisions, habits and actions were more than a little odd.

That said, nothing he did struck her as dangerous. If he'd given off even a hint of trouble, Mom would have avoided him *like the plague*, to use one of her favorite phrases. Just as polar bears can smell seals from miles away, Mom could spot *shady characters* from a similarly impressive distance. Cautious and apprehensive by nature, her anxiety had been stoked by growing up during the 1940s, an era in which people didn't talk openly about taboo subjects. Rape and sexual abuse victims, most of them female, suffered in silence, lest they be labeled *loose* and *asking for it*. Adding to that sense of *you could be next*, her dad traveled for weeks at a time for business. As head of the household, her mom drove home one main survival lesson: *watch out for men because they only want one thing*.

Given Mom's high level of scrutiny about men, it's saying something that Dad not only passed her rigorous safety test but did so with flying colors. Seemingly unaware of his movie-star good looks, he was polite, possessed an absentminded professor demeanor, and went to church every week.

Despite his many good attributes, however, she knew there was a shadowy *something* about him she couldn't put her finger on, as evidenced by phrases she repeated when my sisters and I were kids.

And I remember thinking, what is wrong with him?

He never listens.

It's not worth getting a divorce over.

Your father loves you.

She repeated the last as though to convince us. Yet we didn't need assurance. We knew Dad loved us. What she should have said was, *You don't have to be scared of him.* But maybe, deep down, making that statement risked that she'd see the truth in our young eyes. We were afraid of him. In specific, we were scared of his rare, unpredictable, and frightening outbursts.

Even now, my memory of that youthful reaction strikes me as unfair. My dad lived most of his life as a calm, logical, responsible, loving guy. Yet what I remember are those few, dark moments of seemingly inexplicable rage. Maybe they happened rarely enough to produce a sharp contrast between his normal behavior and those scary instances, enough to forever spotlight those occasions in my otherwise peaceful and happy suburban youth.

Even as kids, my sisters and I knew that everyone, including parents, got upset and yelled on occasion. Our dad even spanked us a few times at Mom's behest after deciding we should be punished for doing something that scared her *half to death*, like wandering off without telling her. At the time, such corporal punishment was an accepted parental tool, so long as parents didn't really hurt their kids. That's what made our spankings oddly normal, scripted, and non-threatening. Dad came home from work. Mom told him what we'd done. Dad came into our room, held us by one arm so our little bodies wouldn't fall over, and gave us a few half-hearted whacks on the bottom. We cried, of course, but mostly because we felt sorry for ourselves. More importantly, we understood the reason for the punishment. We'd done something wrong and our parents felt the need to teach us a lesson.

I would have chosen a dozen spankings over one of Dad's rages, which scared the shit out of me. With no forewarning, he struck fast as a snake, changing from a loving dad into someone almost unable to control himself. Body quivering, light blue eyes narrowed, he'd grip my skinny arm until his fingers touched my bone. Half lifting me off the floor, he'd whisper through gritted teeth, *If you don't be quiet, I'm going to swat you!*

The painful squeeze meant nothing compared to the terrifying way he looked at me, as though he didn't recognize me or remember I was his kid and half his size. Instead, his eyes seemed to hiss, *You're my adversary and if I need to, I'll kill you.* In those moments, I felt he could.

Maybe if he'd come to me afterward and apologized, or at least told me why he'd gotten upset, I might not have feared him. But there never seemed to be a clear reason. Either that or his stated reasons seemed shockingly trivial. My sisters and I could make all kinds of obvious, inconvenient or even expensive mistakes—dropping a plate of food, breaking a tool, getting a flat tire from driving over a curb—and he'd remain calm. Then something so small as to be unseeable would inflame him, like dressing sloppily, despite the fact we dressed like that all the time during our non-school hours, and it was the weekend, and there was no reason to dress up. Another time, he railed at me for wearing red nail polish that was too red, when I regularly painted my nails burgundy, crimson and fuchsia. And once, when our family was down in the basement watching TV, he blew up because Sue didn't get up from where she sat on the floor when Mom bent down to give a goodnight kiss. In those moments, he became a deranged drill sergeant whose entire body would clench into one tight muscle as he yelled, the moment brief, but savage. Afterward, he never explained. Worse, he acted normal, as though nothing had happened.

As a kid, the message was clear. I didn't have a chance of protecting myself. If I hadn't seen the clues leading to the outburst, I wouldn't next time either. Lacking the knowledge of what might send him into a rage or when, I had no way to avoid such incidents and save myself. Though he might not have an outburst for a long time—months, a year, maybe two—during all of that time, I feared the moment he would.

Maybe that's where the true unfairness resides, that in a child's mind, there's little separation between make-believe and reality. My dad was my dad. But after a sudden display of fury, in my mind, he transformed into a sea serpent. And as every kid knows, such monsters remain submerged beneath a still and beautiful surface for long, undisturbed periods of time that tempt you to think you're safe. But if you step even one toe into that water, the serpent can swallow you whole.

—

On the August evening Mom told me the story about Dad, we'd been talking about him in the idle, harmless way family members chat about one another's quirks. Even as we talked, I heard him through the screen door, clumping down the basement steps. Now a man in his seventies, he was finishing a project and not yet ready for the late-night dinner he preferred.

"He's never had a way with kids," Mom said. "You remember that time he picked up Uncle Tom's daughter?"

I smiled and nodded, remembering the incident of twenty years ago when my parents and I visited Dad's mom in her senior living apartment in Alton. Dad's younger brother had come to visit with his wife and six-month-old daughter, who sat wailing in a playpen. Frustrated that my aunt and uncle couldn't soothe

the child, Dad reached down and swung the baby up as if to playfully throw her in the air. She screamed twice as loud. Tom grabbed his daughter.

My dad said, "All she needs is a little distraction."

Through politely gritted teeth, my mom said, "Ray, that scared her!"

Now, so many years later, Mom smiled and shook her head at the memory. "I still remember that scream. Bloody murder! Well, he once did something like that to Sue," she said, referring to my middle sister, who's two years older than me. "This one time, Sue and he were playing in the snow. She had to be, I don't know, maybe only five or six. Anyway, she got all excited and pushed it. You know how she is. I think she threw snow in his face. And oh, the look that came over him."

Mom leaned toward me and mimicked Dad's narrowed eyes and bared teeth with such accuracy my skin crawled.

Dropping the impersonation, Mom leaned back in her chair and said, "And I thought, *Uh-oh*. And then he started rolling her."

"Rolling her?"

"Yeah," and Mom used a finger to demonstrate how a barrel rolls. "Over and over, and poor Sue was so scared and I yelled at him, 'Ray, stop that!' And I got to her, and he stopped."

For a moment, my mind couldn't take in the thought of a grown man becoming so enraged by his six-year-old daughter that he'd roll her in the snow. And yet, my mind immediately filled with the image of Dad doing just that: teeth clenched, lips curled.

"So why did he do something like that?" I said.

"That's what I wondered. When I asked him, he said he saw what she did as a sign of disrespect. He told me, 'My kids are going to respect me, by gum.'"

And Mom nodded as if she understood. As if terrifying your own child by rolling her around in the snow in a fit of anger at a supposed slight is somehow understandable.

"Yeah, but Mom, that's crazy. She was what, five or six?"

"About that."

And I thought, *Poor Sue.*

Though Mom and I sat quietly, the serenity of the evening now felt sinister. What else hid beneath that seemingly tranquil beauty? There was no way Mom would have remembered, much less recalled, an incident from more than forty years ago, not to mention one that shone an unflattering light on a man she always protected, if she hadn't felt his reaction was somehow wrong and inconsistent with the fact that he loved Sue. Yet he'd done that to her.

As I watched bats begin their dusk flight in search of insects—small, quick black darts spearing the air—I thought about Sue and how she must have felt as her dad's powerful hands roughly pushed her small body again and again. The world tumbling as snow filled her mouth, a moment of bliss turning into terror as the man she'd thought would never hurt her emerged as a serpent come to swallow her.

Only years later would my sisters and I decipher the enigma of how a loving, good-hearted man could be a responsible dad one moment, and a monster the next.

Little children

dance among the diamonds
fingertips flung
in sunshine arrays,

bodies light and small, scrambling up the sand
and back again, crab fast

diving amidst the wealth of
unfettered moments,

salted lips puckered, but not yet
embittered

I got a phone call from Sue on a warm May day in 1997.

In my thirties now, I lived in Northern California with my husband, five-year-old daughter and three-year-old son. Both of my sisters had kids roughly the same age. Every week we'd call one another to chat about our lives. Birthday parties. Funny kid anecdotes. Runny noses.

This time, though, the conversation quickly diverged from the mundane.

"Brian was diagnosed with Asperger Syndrome," Sue said.

"What? You're kidding!" I said.

"Unfortunately, I'm not. Go figure."

We were talking about her three-year-old son and a neurological disorder that had only become a named, diagnosable condition a few years previous, in 1994. At the time known as *Asperger's* and described as *high-functioning autism,* the condition had been in the news a lot in the last few years as the number of diagnosed kids continued to climb.

"I don't understand," I said while walking from the kitchen to my patio where my son played in the sandbox.

"Asperger's is—"

"I know what Asperger's *is*," I said, knowing I sounded impatient, when really I felt angry at the universe for placing such a formidable challenge on such a sweet boy.

"Who's *they* and how did they figure it out?" I said. "I mean, are they sure?"

"Yeah, they're sure."

She went on to describe the evaluations completed by various professionals: Brian's preschool teacher, pediatrician, school district psychologist, speech pathologist and occupational therapist. While listening, I walked to the end of my patio and spotted my daughter astride a short fence my husband and I built for climbing.

"So what does this mean exactly?" I said.

Sighing heavily, Sue said, "He's got to go for services. He'll have an aide in the classroom. He'll have an IEP."

"Which is?"

"Individualized Education Plan. It says what services the school district has to provide him, by law. Dee writes them for her kids."

Three years older, Dee was a speech pathologist for a school district. She spent every spring feverishly writing such reports. Most of the kids she worked with were autistic.

"Well, I guess it's good he'll get services," I said.

"I guess," she said, her tone unconvinced.

"I'm glad he's not profound."

"There's that."

From what I'd learned from articles and news programs, profoundly autistic kids often couldn't speak and possessed repetitive habits, some of which were harmful, like banging their heads against a wall. That inability to speak and the odd mannerisms reminded me of my mom's youngest sister, Mary, who had Down Syndrome.

Brian clearly functioned at a higher level. He talked easily and didn't seem to have any overtly unusual behaviors. He had a marvelous personality that included a complete absence of malice, to the point he seemed incapable of lying, excluding others or even speaking cruelly to them. I remember him belly-laughing for hours during a summer picnic as he ran around getting people to sit on a whoopee cushion that made a fake farting sound. If he broke anything while playing, he'd look up at you with guileless green eyes that seemed to ask what went wrong.

Then again, he broke a lot of things.

"So that's why he kicks everything," I said.

"Yup."

Sue had a tidy home until the moment Brian started to walk. From then on, he dented walls, knocked table legs askew, gouged dressers and otherwise kicked what he could and crashed his toys into everything else. Dee later told me the urge to ram things reflected his need for high-impact *stimming*, short for *self-stimulation*.

Most of us have stims, or socially acceptable self-soothing actions such as twirling our hair or tapping our fingers while thinking. But some autistic people have stims that are more obvious, repetitive and socially unacceptable, such as hopping up and down or rocking back and forth. The behaviors can interfere with learning and are often judged as inappropriate by neurotypical (NT) people, or those not affected by a neurological condition, which is why those on the spectrum are often socially shunned. Yet kids like Brian need those stims to self-soothe and release endorphins, a natural painkiller. Often stimming is not a choice but instead triggered by sensory overload, or in Brian's case, under-stimulation. He bashed into things because he craved more sensory input. The thought crossed my mind that maybe when he got a little older, he could start a daily running routine like my dad and find solace in the rhythmic, pounding heel strikes.

I sat down on the patio step to watch my daughter straddle the fence like a cowboy and argue with some invisible cowhand.

"I guess it makes sense, though," I said. "You remember when he was moaning last summer?"

"What do you mean, *moaning?*"

"You remember. We went to that terrible beach with the weird tanker floating offshore in the distance."

"I think that was a garbage barge. That place was so gross."

During my last vacation to the East Coast, my sisters and I drove our kids an hour to a beach on the southern New Jersey shore on a hot day. Only when we schlepped our gear down to the beach did we appreciate why the parking lot was empty. Garbage littered the sand and a grungy *Mad Max*-style barge sat a mile offshore, filling the sea breeze with an unpleasant stink. We would have left immediately, but the kids needed to run around before we put them back in the car.

"Brian got upset, I don't even remember about what," I said. "He like ... wandered away to that retaining wall and lay sideways and moaned."

"Thanks for reminding me," she said.

Sue had tried to soothe him. When I wandered over, she stood. *What's wrong with him?* I'd said. Looking frustrated, she'd tossed a hand, saying, *I have no idea.*

I sat beside him. *What's wrong, Bri?* Then, *You don't want to tell me?* Then, *It's going to be all right.* And finally, *When we leave, we're going for ice cream.* But Brian seemed impervious to my words, soothing tone or attempts to distract him, strategies that worked with my kids. Instead, he continued his repetitive moan in a tone that slid from high to low, all the while staring at the ocean.

"Where does it come from, Asperger's?" I said. "Is it hereditary?"

"They don't know. Nobody has it in our family. I'm worried it might be that medicine I took for the infection I had when I was pregnant with Bri. You remember? When we were visiting you that summer when the girls were little?"

"How far along were you?"

"Three months."

"Yeah, but didn't your doctor say it was okay to take?"

"Yeah, but what do they really know?"

I realized she blamed herself. She often did, having developed a poor self-esteem garnered from her position as a middle child. That and she bore constant criticism from adults—my parents, teachers, bosses—based on behavior caused by her then-undiagnosed Attention Deficit Hyperactivity Disorder (ADHD). The condition, which causes impulsiveness, distraction and disorganization, wasn't officially recognized until the 1990s, long after the damage from her youth had been done. Eventually, six of the eight children my sisters and I bore would be diagnosed with the disorder. But at least by then the condition had a name and we could help our kids understand the challenges and give them strategies developed by educators, doctors and other professionals.

"Oh, come on, Sue, this is not your fault," I said, watching my son wander toward his sister.

"But what if it is?"

"But it's not. This is biology talking. You know how this works. The little egg with all of its baggage meets up with the sperm and all of its shit. The two shake it up, and that's the body chemistry a kid gets stuck with. Maybe this is a case of being chemically unlucky."

"I don't know."

I couldn't insist on being right because I hadn't done any research on the subject. Since graduating in journalism eleven years prior, I'd written a number of medically-oriented articles for a variety of publications, but had never written about autism specifically. While most of the maladies I learned about—cancer, diabetes, arthritis, Meniere's disease—had strong genetic components, I didn't draw the obvious conclusion that autism most likely had a hereditary component too. As a result, I didn't once consider that Mom or Dad could have autism.

I reassured and commiserated with Sue yet did so as someone who believed this was her problem, not mine.

Time and circumstance would soon implode my ordered universe.

subject: jam umm

I just received
the plum jam
you sent.

It really is quite

good.

I must say

that I was

skeptical
at first,

but it was very
tasty.

I thought
your specialty

was salads

not
sweets,

so this must
be a new
avenue

for you.

Well,

so far great

success
thanks
much
love,

1911

Around nineteen years before my dad was born, the world was falling in love with airplanes. The Mexican Revolution took off. The SS Lusitania passenger liner sank. George V was crowned king of Britain.

Amongst that turn-of-the-century mix of human innovation and mayhem, a Swiss psychiatrist named Eugen Bleuler first used the word *autism*. Greek for *autos*, or *self*, as in *self-isolated*, he used the word to describe patients who seemed socially withdrawn, detached from reality and unusually self-absorbed.

In a land far, far away, little five-year-old Margaret Purvis, my dad's mom, went about her day in Alton, IL, a hilly city opposite St. Louis on the Mississippi River. Founded in 1818, the community was home to the very successful Illinois Glass Company.

But Margaret didn't care about any of that. She was five and didn't yet want to be a nun, an aspiration my mom later told me about. Neither Margaret, nor any of her classmates, were assessed for autism because the diagnosis wouldn't exist for another eighty years.

1925

Jewish Soviet child psychiatrist Grunya Sukhareva published a paper in which she described specific symptoms of what she called *autistic psychopathy* based on her observations of boys she studied in a Moscow clinic.

The first symptom was that of a "flattened affective life," meaning a person shows little emotion, even in situations that typically evoke strong emotion in others. That was true of my dad, who would one day deliver life-collapsing one-liners while wearing an expression of mild puzzlement.

The next batch of symptoms speaks to a narrow funnel of awareness: a preference for one's own company; a hyperfocus on, and often talent for, a few interests. In my dad's case, he loved running, fixing things, reading the newspaper and following his investments. All solitary activities that appealed to his logical, fact-loving brain and that gave him a sense of control and firm daily structure.

Sukhareva also noticed that the kids she studied had sensory sensitivities or unusual eating habits. At some point Dad gave up breakfast, then lunch. At midday, he'd imbibe copious amounts of liquids that included juice combinations and hot drinks. His massive dinners consisted of sauces he mixed himself and spooned over whatever food Mom made. He mixed powdered Jell-O mix into his milk and poured whole cans of condensed canned tomato soup on his salad. Many of his habits were based on theories he'd formed after reading newspaper articles about the latest health research, especially those that involved increasing one's lifespan.

The last symptom Sukhareva listed was that of social awkwardness. Though friendly and polite, my dad didn't have friends other than Mom because he found friendships too time-consuming and disruptive of his schedule. Driven by a strong sense of duty—his perception of what he should do as a good son, father, husband and Catholic—he good-naturedly took part in social activities involving church and school functions. He even starred in our church's production of *South Pacific*.

Since kids didn't hang out with adults back then, I don't know what social gaffes he might have made other than the two I know about. Mom once told me when she and Dad were playing doubles tennis with another couple, he got so mad about making an error that he broke his racket. Mortified, Mom quietly withdrew them from the league. The second instance occurred when an old Army buddy and his family came to visit. As the adults talked and we kids listened, Dad made a joke about the man's obesity. Though I was only about eight years old, I knew Dad had just made a big social faux pas and glanced around to see other expressions that reflected the awkward moment. Yet Dad seemed unaware he was the only one who laughed. Mom, his faithful assistant, smoothed over the moment by offering a more socially acceptable interpretation.

Dad possessed other symptoms that would later be identified as autistic, such as his adherence to a rigid schedule. Another would be the rages we witnessed, otherwise known as *meltdowns* that stemmed from an overload of sensory input. That's as opposed to tantrums thrown by allistic (non-autistic) people frustrated by not getting what they want. Lastly, Dad had difficulty with perspective-taking, the neurological ability to put yourself in someone else's shoes to approximate how they might feel and so empathize with them.

Regarding Sukhareva's research, Lina Zeldovich stated in her article, *How History Forgot the Woman Who Defined Autism* (*Spectrum* 2018):

> At first, Sukhareva used "autistic" in the same way Bleuler did—but as she started to see other children with this trait, she decided to try to characterize it

more fully. Over the course of the following year, she identified five more boys with what she described as "autistic tendencies." All five also showed a preference for their own inner world, yet each had his own peculiarities or talents. One was an extraordinarily gifted violinist but struggled socially; another had an exceptional memory for numbers but could not recognize faces; yet another had imaginary friends who lived in the fireplace. None were popular with other children, she noted, and some saw peer interaction as useless: "They are too loud," one boy said. "They hinder my thinking."

As Sukhareva continued her research, nineteen-year-old Margaret apparently decided, at the behest of her mother, to forgo the ordered world of the nunnery. Instead, my grandma became a secretary at the Illinois Glass Company where she met a factory worker named Andy Podhorn.

1930

The Jewish-Austrian psychiatrist Leo Kanner immigrated to the US to take a position at Johns Hopkins Hospital in Maryland, where he founded the first child psychiatry clinic in the country.

By then, though the field had progressed, diagnostic tools were still rudimentary, terms imprecise and knowledge scarce. People either developed normally or there was something wrong with them. When obvious, that wrongness led to commonly-used derogatory nicknames: *cripples, dimwits, the feeble-minded, maniacs.* If people looked normal, but were slightly off, people said exactly that, *There's something off about him,* or *he's eccentric, touched,* or *quirky.*

Back in Alton, the Illinois Glass Company merged with Owens to become Owens-Illinois Glass Company. Assured of work and financial security, Margaret and Andy married in June of 1929.

I've only seen one photo of my grandma's wedding. Bathed in sepia tones, Grandma sits on a chair with her ankles crossed in a ladylike manner. She wears a 1920s-style white tea-length dress and a long veil. Two nameless women sit beside her, one on either side. Behind the women stand my grandpa and two men. I imagine the event to be a simple affair. The relatives come. The priest pronounces the couple man and wife. Guests are offered some refreshments served in the church basement. Then the newlyweds go home to start their life together.

Three months later, on October 29, the stock market crashed and the Great Depression began. Bonnie and Clyde, a pair of twenty-something robbers and murderers, alternately terrorized and inspired the masses in nearby Missouri, Oklahoma, Indiana and Texas.

Nine months later, on July 21, 1930, Margaret gave birth to my dad, Raymond, the first of five kids.

I'd like to say she told me stories about my grandpa, who died when I was little, or about my dad and aunts and uncle, but she never did. She didn't mention funny memories or family get-togethers. When she came to visit for a month at a time, she read the newspaper, practiced bridge and cooked delicious food: fried chicken, mashed potatoes, apple pie. She played cards with us kids, made fudge and washed her hair with eggs. She spoke politely to other adults about socially acceptable topics such as the weather, though at times, and maybe like most of us, she'd drop quiet, awkward one-liners. *You've put on a little weight.* Or she'd squeeze my arm, muscled from various activities, and say, *Good arm*, at a time when a strong female physique was not desirable.

After meeting Sue's fiancé, Grandma said, *He's backwards.* Sue said, *What?* Grandma amended her comment to, *He's shy.*

Not without a sense of humor, she once told us about talking with a woman who had a big nose. Grandma fixated on the feature until at some point she called the woman *Miss Nose.* We all laughed.

1938

In 1938, Kanner began observing three girls and eight boys who had what he described as *infantile autism,* having borrowed the term from Bleuler. Kanner began to see a new syndrome occur, one separate from intellectual disabilities or schizophrenia and that included a disruption of social and language development.

"The core elements of the phenotype that Kanner highlighted included a profound lack of affective contact with others, an anxiously obsessive desire for the preservations of sameness, a monotonous repetition of verbal and motor behavior, a fascination for objects, and mutism or language that did not seem intended to serve the purpose of interpersonal communication," states *Update on Diagnostic Classification in Autism* (Bryan King, Noa Navot, Raphael Bernier, Sara Jane Webb, *Current Opinion in Psychiatry*, March 2014, Vol. 27, Issue 2).

During this time, I imagine rigorous discussions taking place among a small number of academics and researchers regarding this baffling condition. They wrote articles and letters for one another. They attended conferences nobody paid attention to other than those in the field of child psychiatry.

Now contrast that with bigger, flashier happenings. Orson Welles aired his now infamous fictional radio drama, *The War of the Worlds*, based on the H. G. Wells's novel of the same name. Within hours of realistic reporting and terrifying sound effects, Welles and his fellow actors managed to convince millions of Americans that Martians had landed in New Jersey and were systematically wiping out humanity. One of those scared listeners was my eight-year-old dad. He later told us about running to his mother and pleading with her to flee before the aliens came. But she was painting the bathroom, and after that, had more chores to do, so she said, *That's ridiculous. No aliens are coming. Go wash up for dinner.*

I can only imagine what eight-year-old Ray might have been like. A loner, but a busy one, always moving and learning. If others noted his tendency for solitude, they probably didn't think much about it. Some people were just that way, just as others might be *rabble-rousers* or *smooth-talkers.* If anyone noted his fascination for tools, they probably would have ascribed the appeal as normal for a boy and indicative of a bright future for such an industrious mind.

I assume at least a few of them would smile kindly at the future image of a man who'd one day be so enamored of fix-it materials that when he ventured to the hardware store, his wife would send at least one of his three daughters with him to make sure he didn't stay for hours. In truth, my sisters and I didn't mind going since most of the time we could talk Dad into buying us treats.

1943

After five years of observing child patients, Kanner published his paper titled *Autistic Disturbances of an Affective Contact.* He described their need for "extreme aloneness," their great rote memories, and their need to engage in repetitive behaviors.

Now thirteen, my dad at some point had an ear infection that went untreated long enough to cause lasting hearing loss in his left ear. He got his first job as an attendant at a filling station where you could buy gas for fifteen cents a gallon and Coca-Cola for five cents. Prohibition over, parents could send their kids to buy a bucket of beer at the local tavern. The average cost of a new home was $3,600. World War II necessitated the rationing of shoes, canned goods, cheese, and meat. Dwight Eisenhower became the Supreme Allied Commander, and the Nazis wiped out the Jewish ghetto in Krakow, Poland.

During this time, some kid broke my dad's arm. The few times Dad mentioned such bullying, he said his lack of height made him a target. That and the culture of his era and locale expected boys to *roughhouse* and in the process they would learn to defend themselves. Mom later told us that what Dad didn't like about getting picked on was feeling disrespected, which might have led to his tendency to misinterpret situations as displays of contempt, as he'd one day do when his six-year-old daughter threw snow in his face.

Almost sixty years would pass before the Interactive Autism Network (IAN) would release data from a survey of American Autism Spectrum Disorder (ASD) kids stating a whopping 61% of low-support needs autistic kids like my nephew reported being bullied, as opposed to 12% of neurotypical kids. (*IAN Research Report: Bullying and Children With ASD*, March 2012).

From today's perspective, the reasons ASD kids get bullied seem obvious. Despite having an extremely difficult time socializing, they're thrown in with kids who have the advantage of observing—and exploiting—others' oddities. Adolescent neurotypicals are quick to discover that ASD kids interpret colloquialisms literally—*Go jump off a cliff? Why would I do that?*—which

NT teens might find not only hilarious but also convenient for inciting those on the spectrum.

For better or worse, the bullying Dad endured during his adolescence taught him to stand up for himself. And during that time, school proved to be a saving grace. He soaked up what he learned. Possessing a fantastic rote memory, he became a great analytical thinker who found solace in reason and logic. Throughout his life he could reference what he'd read: hundreds of nonfiction books and articles on history, religion, investments and science. Even in the month before he died, my sisters marveled at how he could recall the exact year various medieval wars began. As an amateur scholar, he was a *sharp cookie*, as Mom used to say.

1944

A year later, Austrian pediatrician Hans Asperger published a paper that included descriptions of autism similar to those published by Sukhareva two decades before, though he didn't credit her. A eugenicist, Asperger believed the human race could be improved by excluding inferior groups of people, which dovetailed well with the Nazi mentality.

Asperger made his observations while working with autistic kids at a Vienna clinic. He encouraged those children to be included in school if they weren't too affected. But if they had a more severe form of disability, he sent them to a clinic that performed experiments and euthanasia on patients (*Asperger's Children: The Origins of Autism in Nazi Vienna*, Edith Sheffer, 2018).

The four boys he studied for his paper seemed to exhibit a lack of empathy, an inability to form relationships, the habit of talking in monologues rather than participating in the back-and-forth exchange of ideas known as conversation and the ability to hyperfocus on a particular subject. He followed at least one of the kids to adulthood and observed that the man's extremely astute focus on astronomy allowed him to become very successful in his career.

At fourteen, my dad had three younger sisters and a brother. I don't know much about Dad's childhood because he rarely talked about his upbringing. I can't remember him mentioning his father more than a few times. Like Grandma Margaret, he didn't tell stories about his brothers or sisters either, except for a few anecdotes about when he and his brother bicycled across France either during or after his Army days. And the only story he told about his family was when his mom got a wild hair to see the Wisconsin Dells and pestered her husband until he gave in. Having never taken a long-distance trip, they failed to plan. The family piled in the car, drove north for hours without a map, and when night came, stopped at a park where Dad remembered sleeping on a picnic table, his empty stomach growling. The next day they drove home.

Once a year Dad took us to visit his mother, during which we'd see two of his sisters and their families, who lived in the area. Very occasionally we'd visit his brother and his family, whereas his third sister I only saw twice. Though he kept up with his siblings to some degree through phone calls and letters, he never relayed any news. Instead, extended-family happenings got passed along through Mom, who wrote and received yearly Christmas cards. In contrast, my sisters and I knew my mom's side of the family well and went to visit them in upstate New York during summer vacation. That contrast between how much we knew about Mom's extended family made me suspect something was amiss—or missing—in the dynamics between my dad and his family. I knew they existed, but their presence felt vague. Had we known them better, we might have learned about genetic issues that showed up over time, whether cancer, ADHD or autism.

Just as my dad didn't tell us much about his youth, I gradually and mostly unconsciously gave up trying to tell him about myself. He just didn't seem to be interested. Even as an adult, whenever I called home, Mom would put Dad on the line. He'd ask a few basic questions about my health and welfare, and I'd assure him I was fine. Then he'd tell me something of interest he read in *The Wall Street Journal*. Sometimes I'd try to respond, but by the way he interrupted or asked me to repeat what I said, he clearly couldn't hear me. I assumed his hearing loss was the reason he talked in monologues. I rarely bothered to offer an opinion or to tell him about my life other than basic news because he didn't know enough about me to make the effort worthwhile. Rather than feel bitter, those moments on the phone with Dad struck me as normal.

1952

The American Psychiatric Association published the *Diagnostic and Statistical Manual of Mental Disorders.* Meant to help clinicians diagnose patients based on research and agreed-upon terms, the publication included descriptions and symptoms of mental disorders along with assessment criteria.

Now twenty-two, my dad was in the Army. He never told us about his experience other than a few amusing anecdotes, though I can only imagine the harassment he must have faced as a short, earnest young man neurologically wedded to logic and literalness. He became a lieutenant at the tail end of the Korean War and after the fighting ceased, traveled the countryside. Fascinated by everything he saw, he took dozens of photos of farmers in their fields; images he never showed us but that we later found in a box. Up to this point in his life, he hadn't traveled much beyond Illinois. The idea of a vacation was still a relatively new concept in America. Many families like his didn't have the financial wherewithal for such an extravagance. When Dad got this first look at a wider world, he immediately developed a passion for trips that allowed him to indulge his love of learning. The idea of visiting the same locale twice, or remaining in one place just to relax, would forever be concepts he couldn't understand.

1967

Autism was officially classified in the *International Statistical Classification of Diseases and Related Health Problems* under schizophrenia. This was an era of psychoanalysis which encouraged autism researchers to focus on life experiences that might cause the disorder. Psychologist Bruno Bettelheim claimed autism was caused by "refrigerator moms" who didn't love their kids enough.

Now thirty-seven, my dad had a bachelor's degree in English thanks to the GI Bill after which he taught high school English for three years. He mentioned the latter experience years later during one of my summer visits. I sat at the breakfast bar, watching him wander around, getting his dinner. He pulled a box of crackers from the pantry, microwaved his juice, shook raisins into his salad and mixed prune juice into his bran cereal.

"So why did you quit teaching?" I said.

A pained expression crossed his face as he backhanded the air in a gesture of frustration. "The students were so lazy," he said. "They didn't want to learn. You'd try to talk to them, and they weren't interested." He shook his head.

I nodded, all the while deeply empathizing with his students. During my school years, I could tell the difference between teachers who really want to hear what their students have to say and teachers who tell kids what they should think. Dad belonged to the latter. The situation must have been doubly frustrating for him because if he loved a subject, he couldn't understand why others didn't. Lastly, he had a hard time loosening up and just having fun. On the few occasions he took my sisters and me bowling, we looked forward to laughing at gutter balls and otherwise telling jokes and talking smack about one another. Dad, on the other hand, took the opportunity to give us pointers and expressed frustration if we didn't try harder.

If working with others wasn't his strong point, he was very good at analyzing data. When he embarked on a master's degree in business administration, he chose correctly. He became a systems analyst, first at IBM during its youth, then at the Federal Reserve Bank in Chicago. In 1960, he married my mom, Norma Mae Duffany, a special education teacher who taught blind kids until quitting to have children, first Deanna and then Susan, followed by me in 1964.

In 1967, I was three and we lived in Mom's mother's red house in Naperville on the outskirts of suburban Chicago. While I knew my parents loved us girls and were always around somewhere, I relied on my sisters—my best buddies—for comfort.

1977

A study published in the *Journal of Child Psychology and Psychiatry* that involved twenty-one pairs of British twins found that autism is mostly hereditary. A study published in the July 17, 2019, issue of *JAMA Psychiatry*, which involved two million people in five countries, corroborated that finding, stating heredity is 80% responsible for the disorder. The remaining 20% is due to as-yet-undiscovered environmental factors.

While autism shares a number of traits with narcissism, the two are different in significant ways. The latter is a personality disorder, rather than a neurological condition, in which people have an exaggerated view of their superiority. Though self-absorbed and lacking empathy, narcissists are aware of hurting others, but either don't care or actually delight in the act. Those with ASD, on the other hand, would prefer not to hurt others' feelings, but like my dad, often lack the perspective-taking necessary to see when they might be doing so.

In 1978, psychologists David Premack and Guy Woodruff coined the phrase *theory of mind* (ToM) to describe that ability to put oneself in another's shoes. Doing so allows us to predict how people will act. A lack of ToM is called *mind blindness*.

By this time, Dad and Mom bought a house in the Chicago suburb of La Grange, IL, based on the home's proximity to the Burlington Northern Railroad line. Now in his late forties, Dad took the train to and from work in Chicago. When he got home, he changed out of his suit, we ate dinner, and then he fixed things. He took out, or put in, winter storm windows. He replaced cracked caulking around the bathtub. He plugged leaking sinks.

I was everything a twelve-year-old girl should be: braces, acne, touchy when criticized, overly romantic. I had a high need to move and had already taken seven years of tap dance, but I really wanted to take ballet at the prestigious Chicago ballet school my neighbor attended. Often feeling the need to let off steam, I danced around the basement to music from my mom's extensive collection of musicals: *Kismet, South Pacific, The King and I.*

I talked as much as necessary to be sociable with those I didn't know well. I had a small group of friends at school and took part in every performance-oriented activity I could: choir, dance, plays. If I had a problem, I bypassed Mom, who worried easily and, in my adolescent opinion, made too much of everything. Instead, I turned to my sisters when I was bored, happy, frustrated or sad, when I needed a ride somewhere, or when I needed to borrow money or clothes.

Sue baked the muffins, banana bread, cookies and other goodies my sweet tooth demanded and my healthy-minded, perpetually-dieting mom refused to buy. On summer days too hot to be outside, Sue and I sat thigh-to-thigh in the cool basement, watching old movies on TV. When her pet gerbil, Herman, died, I sat with her as she cried and cried. Though emotionally volatile, she was always so generous and forthright that I knew where she stood at any given moment.

Dee noted my mood changes, much as I tried to hide them, like the day I walked in after school, stomped upstairs and disappeared into my room. She followed me in, curled up with me on my bed and encouraged me to talk about the humiliation I'd suffered during a dance team audition at school. Possessing a calm demeanor, she could put my fears into perspective until they dwindled in size and intensity.

The three of us kidded each other about farts and burps. We pulled together when Dad yelled at us suddenly for no apparent reason. We defended one another from bullies, whether kids at school or critical adults. We sang in the choir and played soft-ball in a teen league. We walked in Morten's Arboretum on a gorgeous fall day, singing the theme to *The Monkees* TV show while inserting our ridiculous last name.

> Here we come, walkin' down the street
> We get the funniest looks from every one we meet
> Hey, hey, we're the Podhorns and people say we monkey around
> But we're too busy singing to put anybody down

Don't get me wrong. My sisters and I argued plenty, got jealous of one another and slugged each other from time to time. But if you'd been able to crawl inside any of us, you would have seen the invisible stitches that bound our hearts together. My sisters were—and are—my team, my crew, my war heroes.

In contrast, I never considered talking to Dad about anything personal. Doing so would have been strange, like entering a store for the sole purpose of telling my innermost feelings to the clerk. Someone who doesn't know me. Someone who doesn't understand what I'm talking about. Someone who strongly doubts sharing feelings has any practical purpose, but who possesses enough kindness to listen and tell me what he'd do in my situation.

My mom, sisters and I knew he didn't seem to understand his own feelings either. When frustrated or stressed, he lashed out in odd ways. Once he criticized Sue, then a teenager, for what he considered a disheveled appearance. He ended by suggesting she put a bow in her hair. Bizarre advice, considering she was not only long past the days of little girl bows, but she had short hair. When I lost a windbreaker during my first-ever date and the boy kindly bought me another jacket with my name emblazoned in five-inch letters across the back, Dad insisted on paying for the item. He went so far as to follow the dude out of the house to force him to take the reimbursement. The implication of his action was painfully obvious to the rest of us, that unless he compensated this boy for the $12 expenditure, I'd feel obligated to have sex as a means of repayment.

At about this time, Mom was diagnosed with a brain tumor and underwent two surgeries within a two-week period, the first to cut out the growth and the second to excise a piece that got left behind. One night during this stressful time, Sue went out with friends for the evening. When she didn't arrive home, Dad asked Dee and I about her whereabouts, all in his scary-calm, narrow-eyed way. We said we didn't know, but we understood she would really *get it* when she got home. I hid in my bedroom, praying he wasn't going to hit her, which he'd never done before, but that now seemed possible. Only moments after I heard the front door open and close, I heard Dad yelling. I ran partway down the stairs and bent over the railing. He stood in the foyer, his face two inches from Sue's, barking like a drill sergeant threatening court martial. She stood tall, her face calm. She nodded and kept her voice calm. *Yes. I'm sorry. It won't happen again.* To pacify the man who would have, if he could have, rolled her in the snow again.

1980-81

"Infantile autism" was separated from schizophrenia in the *Diagnostic and Statistical Manual of Mental Disorders.* To that point,

Hans Asperger's research had gone unnoticed. Then in a paper written in 1981, British autism expert Lorna Wing coined the phrase "Asperger syndrome" along with the concept of an autism spectrum. The mother of a severely autistic daughter, Wing introduced three autism subgroups: active-but-odd people, like my dad, those who are passive, and others who are rigid.

Frustrated by getting overlooked for promotion time and again, my dad accepted a transfer to the New York City Federal Reserve Bank, and we moved from Chicago to New Jersey. A year later, I graduated. At the age of seventeen, I left home for the Midwest to pursue a journalism degree at the University of Missouri-Columbia.

1991

The US government classified autism as a special education category and public schools began identifying kids on the spectrum and providing them with services.

I lived with my husband in the Chicago area again. My sisters and parents lived on the East Coast.

Though my parents lived in New Jersey for a few decades before moving to Connecticut, Mom and Dad never rebuilt the social life they'd had in the Midwest. During that earlier time when actively parenting my sisters and me, Dad and Mom interacted socially as a Norma-Ray duo during church functions. They participated in a gourmet dinner club where everyone traveled to each other's homes for various courses. They played tennis in a doubles league until the broken-racket incident.

After moving to the East Coast, my dad didn't seem to miss any of that socializing, whereas Mom felt isolated in their nondescript condo complex. That changed when my sisters and I started having kids, an immediate source of joy for her. By 1991, she had four grandchildren.

1993-94

Asperger's became an official diagnosis and was added to the *International Statistical Classification of Diseases and Related Health Problems 10th revision* (ICD-10) in 1993 and the *Diagnostic and Statistical Manual of Mental Disorders 4th revision* (DSM-IV) in 1994.

Now sixty-four, Dad had seven grandchildren. A year later, he had an eighth and final grandchild. My husband and I had moved to California and had two kids. During my summer visits, Dad remained on the sidelines but clearly loved watching the kids. He laughed and laughed at their many antics.

1997-98

In 1997, I got that phone call from Sue in which she told me her son, Brian, had been diagnosed with Asperger's. Two years later, her second son, Sean, was diagnosed with Pervasive Developmental Disorder (PDD), another form of autism.

When hearing about Sean, I thought, *What the hell? How can her family be that unlucky?*

Sue and her husband again launched into getting three-year-old Sean enrolled in speech and other services, a process they now knew so well. Over the next few years, Sue's tone of voice and increasingly frequent stories of her sons' behavioral troubles and the difficulties of getting services made clear the emotional and physical stress of rearing two kids on the spectrum.

During a phone call in which Sue recounted the latest trouble, she said, "I'm going to write a book about all of this."

Presumably, most parents of challenged kids make such statements, though more out of frustration than actual resolve. And like my sister, they want to help other parents navigate a confusing system. Though I never expected my already time-strapped sister to undertake such a time-consuming project, I nevertheless voiced my support and offered my professional skills if and when she needed them.

By this point, her sons were two among thousands of kids recently diagnosed with ASD, a precipitous increase largely due to the emergence of an actual diagnosis accompanied by the development and subsequent use of more rigorous diagnostic tools. While Sue and her husband understood the idea that if you go looking for something specific, you're more likely to find it, they and thousands of other parents couldn't help but wonder if something else might be causing the seemingly epidemic upswing.

British gastroenterologist Andrew Wakefield took advantage of the situation. While trying to get a patent for his own vaccine, he did a small study in which he concluded the measles, mumps, and rubella vaccine (MMR) caused autism. Though quickly debunked, the falsehood took root among heartbroken parents looking to place blame. Wakefield's erroneous study led to the rise of the anti-vaccination movement that persists to this day.

Now two decades after Mom's surgery to remove a brain tumor, she again began experiencing blinding headaches. Tests concluded the same tumor had slowly regrown. She had another surgery, and despite a bumpy post-op, appeared to recover.

2009

The number of autism cases continued to rise due to better screening and diagnostic tools. The US Centers for Disease Control and Prevention (CDC) estimated one in about a hundred kids had ASD, up from one in a hundred-and-fifty kids in 2007.

Mom's left hip began to bother her. She optimistically offered every excuse: a pulled muscle, arthritis, a too-rigorous walk or bike ride. When the pain became excruciating, she went for tests that concluded some of the cancer cells from her brain tumor had gotten loose during her last surgery. The metastasized cancer now roamed freely and had attached to the hip, though more tumors were probably growing in yet-to-be-discovered locations.

2012

In America, experts reversed their thinking. Rather than giving Asperger Syndrome its own category, the condition got tucked back under the general heading of ASD. Elsewhere in the world, the term Asperger Syndrome remains in use. That disagreement in classification continues to make getting estimates about the number of low-needs autistic people difficult. CDC analysis of data between 2000 and 2018 estimates there are at least seventy-five million people with ASD worldwide, which represents one percent of the world's population.

Though Dad loved Mom passionately, he acted against her best interest time and again and seemed unaware of how his behavior negatively impacted her, especially during her last and worst year of cancer treatment.

When I visited three months before her death, Mom almost died. One day she was fine, and the next she grew drowsy and hard to rouse. We called a visiting nurse, who assumed Mom had begun the active dying process, given her weak pulse and advanced stage of cancer. But on a hunch, the nurse gave Mom liquids, which revived her within an hour. Apparently Mom's numerous prescribed medications made her loopy enough she forgot to drink. After that, we tracked how much she drank.

After another month, however, she lost the ability to swallow. Dad insisted she drink, which made her gag and choke. My sisters explained that rather than flow down her throat to her stomach, the fluids filled her lungs, further depleting her oxygen supply. But Dad couldn't imagine the inability to swallow. And if he could push himself to do things he found unpleasant, why couldn't she? Lastly, he didn't want her to die and seemed compelled to do whatever necessary to keep her alive.

The dying process can be cruel, so we understood Dad's distress and desperation at the thought of losing his best friend. But at some point, his odd behavior grew too pronounced to ignore. His inability to deviate from theories about what might save her, his lack of understanding about what would make her more comfortable, and his growing distress at the disruption of his schedule pointed to a greater problem. Dementia didn't seem to be an issue, given that his cognitive abilities remained high. Upon further contemplation of his unusual habits, we began to suspect Dad had undiagnosed ASD.

His preference for being alone.

His adherence to a rigid daily regimen that included an equally rigid fitness, nutrition and eating schedule.

His tendency to talk in monologues rather than participate in conversations.

His rare, but scary, meltdowns.

His inability to show much affection.

His inability to put himself in others' shoes.

His lack of any friends other than Mom.

In retrospect, the signs now seemed ridiculously obvious. Yet there was no way we could have come to that conclusion any sooner. The diagnosis had only been around for about twenty years, during which the social and scientific emphasis had been on diagnosing children. The concept of undiagnosed adults had yet to emerge as its own phenomenon. That, and my sisters and I didn't have any other dad against whom to compare him. We were used to his oddities. When he did something unusual but harmless, like painting the station wagon with house paint and a brush or patching his old running shoes to the point they looked like two boats of dried shoe glue, we'd smile at one another and warm-heartedly acknowledge, *Yup, that's our dad.* With time and distance, we'd forgotten the frustration of trying to communicate with him about something important.

Only when faced with the prospect of losing the one person to whom he'd bonded did his harmless eccentricities transform into sharp-tipped claws he swiped at Mom and my sisters, her two main caregivers.

Despite his attempts to save her, Mom died in December 2012.

2015

According to a compilation of data between 2000 and 2016, the CDC stated in *Data and Statistics on Autism Spectrum Disorder*:

- one in fifty-four kids is on the spectrum, a statistic that may differ worldwide and be low due to underreporting

- the neurological divergence crosses all racial, ethnic and socioeconomic groups
- the condition is more than four times as prevalent in boys than in girls: one in thirty-seven boys, one in a hundred-and-fifty girls. In 2020, then nineteen-year-old Paige Layle began challenging those statistics by posting short videos asserting Asperger's females like her go undetected because they're better at observing and mimicking social behavior. Maybe that's what happened in the case of my Grandma Margaret, if indeed she had the neurological condition.

Kids on the spectrum can now be diagnosed between fifteen to eighteen months after birth, though the average age is four-and-a-half years. A variety of experts are involved, including psychologists, pediatricians, neurologists, speech pathologists and occupational therapists. The diagnostic process is lengthy and involves patient interviews, behavioral observations, and cognitive, language, and medical tests to rule out other conditions. There are also interviews with parents, teachers and other adults familiar with the patient's social, emotional and behavioral development.

The focus remained—and remains—on identifying and helping kids with autism and their families, rather than on the kids of ASD parents.

2019

My dad died. He had a smooth exit compared to my mom's, mostly because no one interfered as he'd done when she died. My sisters listed his options and let him determine his end. He'd had numerous visits to the emergency room within the last several months to treat a similar aspiration problem to the one Mom experienced. Somewhere in his swallowing process, liquid and food got diverted to his lungs, creating bacteria that led to pneumonia. After numerous bouts with infection, he registered for hospice rather than face more treatment for an incurable problem.

On his final day, my sisters administered the hospice medication necessary to keep him calm and pain-free. They surrounded him with love, music and visits from his grandchildren, making the end-of-life event as beautiful as possible. My sisters called me in California when I happened to be on a work break. As I sat in a coffee shop surrounded by music and people and chatter, they held the phone to his ear and I said goodbye and *I love you*. My sisters said he mouthed the same. *I love you.*

longing

you're standing
on a road,
open,
alone,

feet spread
on the indifference
of crushed
rock

the sun beats,

a heated wind
serpentines
the broken
white
line

making love
to the wide
horizon,

a far distance from
which you can't
divert
your eyes

because of what
could come
rising

toward you,
to you,
at you,
in you

as a dying
breeze fingers soft
blades of hair
across your brow

you narrow-eye
that forever,

a place of undulation
and earth curvature,

of a bare, rippling
back, the contours
of which
you'll
never
know

a fact
that cracks
your scorched
lips
open,

to bleed
a blade tip
slip
of
oh

Dad's Eulogy
by Deanna Rozak

Our dad was a man of many accomplishments and interests. He was a man of learning, charity, action, adventure, integrity and humility. I didn't always understand him when I was young. He was the guy who kept everything quietly running in the background of our lives. Like most dads of that time, he didn't make a big deal about what he contributed and he didn't show a lot of PDA (public displays of affection), which as a child could have been mistaken for him not caring, but he knew that my mom was the affectionate one and he was the guy who needed to provide the stability in our lives.

He was big on going to church and being involved in volunteer work, and he learned to put his money where his mouth was when it came to giving back without letting others know what he was doing. He followed that teaching all his life and gave to over two hundred charities every year. He believed in education and made sure that we all went to college, and he also believed in being physically fit and again taught us by example as a lifelong runner. He taught us about marriage in his relationship with my mom, who was the love of his life for whom he wrote an original poem for almost every one of her birthdays and their anniversaries. He believed in the transformative power of travel and took us on many a summer adventure across country in our station wagon, which inevitably broke down at some point, usually leaving us stranded in some dusty town with one mechanic.

I feel grateful to have had the chance to get to know him over the last few years after my mother died. He had an amazing memory and could remember the title and usually author of books that he had read in college! During our conversations, he would often casually mention some amazing thing that we had never heard before, such as when he met and introduced himself to Harry Truman! We were constantly amazed by the breadth of his knowledge on many topics from history to the stock market. He had a hard time accepting help as he got older and would often try to compensate us for things we did for him by saying, "I want you to go out for dinner, my treat." I know he appreciated all that we did and he would always end our conversations by saying, "Love you." I will miss hearing that and I will miss him beginning his conversations with "Hello, Deann, this is Papa," as if I might not be sure who it was. He was a man who lived by his word, and my sisters and I have tried to do the same. He was quite the character, as anyone who knew him could tell you, but he tried to be the best person he could be every day and I will always admire and love him for the effort.

So goodbye Dad and thanks for everything!

Part II
Me

Box

Piercing tips pointing from every perimeter tower, to keep the
unwanted out and in—
      mates in

By the time my dad died, hundreds of studies had been done about every aspect of autism. Dozens of books had been published for parents of autistic kids to help them cope and prosper. Books by autistic people gave firsthand descriptions of the formidable challenges they faced and what needs to be done to protect those on the spectrum from bullying and discrimination. The U.S. Department of Health and Human Services hosts a directory of organizations aimed at research, self-advocacy, educational programs, and the launch of a Neurodiverse Federal Workforce Pilot Program which "seeks to increase high-tech career opportunities within the federal government for individuals on the autism spectrum by providing a modified application and interview process, professional development coaching, and co-worker autism awareness training."

As a minority population, there's no question how many challenges ASD people face when held against the standards of the non-autistic majority. The latter often doesn't understand the condition, get frustrated by the differences in neural processing, and doesn't yet realize autism is just one of the more recent discoveries about how we're all neurologically different.

In *Unmasking Autism: Discovering the New Faces of Neurodiversity*, Dr. Devon Price, an autistic social psychologist, writes:

> Autism is just one source of *neurodiversity* in our world. The term *neurodiverse* refers to the wide spectrum of individuals whose thoughts, emotions,

or behaviors have been stigmatized as unhealthy, abnormal, or dangerous ... The label neurodiverse includes everyone from people with ADHD, to Down Syndrome, to Obsessive-Compulsive Disorder, to Borderline Personality Disorder.

The list of known neurological conditions goes on to include hundreds of other disorders, from learning disabilities like dyslexia to cognitive deterioration like Alzheimer's to brain injuries, strokes, Carpal Tunnel Syndrome, epilepsy and a variety of mental illnesses, including depression. All of which means, if I were tested and diagnosed with ADHD, I'd be neurodiverse too.

"Essentially no one lives up to the neurotypical standards all of the time," Dr. Price writes. The statement seems to align with the World Health Organization's estimate that hundreds of millions of people have some kind of neurological condition.

That argues for making greater efforts to help not only ASD people overcome societal bias, but to promote the idea of neurodiversity as the new "normal."

After discovering how far researchers have come regarding autism research and other neurological conditions including anxiety, I expected to find research on the possible psychological effects experienced by the allistic children of ASD parents, like me and my sisters.

I found nothing. No studies. No data. No psychologists who specialize in challenges that face the kids of ASD parents.

One of the few tangential studies I found was published in 2016 by researchers at the University of Washington, who determined kids' self-esteem—their evaluation of their own worth—develops by the age of five.

I also found an article written by psychologist Mark Hutten, author of *The Asperger's Comprehensive Handbook:*

Again, no one has studied the impact of Asperger's on parent-child development, but anecdotal evidence suggests these kids need counseling around some of the Asperger's behaviors they grow up with. If we look at an example of one pattern of parental Asperger's behavior one can see how this impacts: Mind blind parents have difficulty distinguishing whether their youngster's actions are intentional or accidental. This is huge for a youngster over the course of years. Non-autistic parents face this dilemma at times, but not in the manner or degree of the Asperger's parent. This one small piece adds enormous dysfunction to these families.

I read that fragment several times: *Difficulty distinguishing whether their youngster's actions are intentional or accidental.* Like when a father tumbles his six-year-old daughter in the snow because he can't distinguish between a child who means to disrespect him and one who's simply overexcited.

That got me thinking.

What if a kid's self-worth gets snipped at the outset of life?

What if that kid's parent lacks the ability to emotionally connect, which in turn impedes, or completely shuts down, the child's emotional development?

What if both of those occur long before the kid learns how to speak?

The answer seemed simple and obvious: there would be no way for anyone to detect a problem.

The kid wouldn't have the words or brain development to understand the concepts involved. The undiagnosed parent wouldn't know his unseen condition might negatively impact his kid's self-esteem. Such a foundational crack would get buried and remain invisible beneath an outwardly normal-looking life.

Like mine.

Elfin Soul

My-
self
      shelved
      elf-
      in soul

I have no way of knowing what happened to me before my memory developed. None of us do, which I find disquieting. Why would evolution favor a lack of memory at that critical period of brain development when we're most vulnerable to others?

That vulnerability becomes painfully apparent when we meet older people who launch into a story, often embarrassing, about what we did when we were too young to remember. We listen, wearing a pained expression because we were there, but not there. We don't know what happened and so can't argue with their claims.

Similarly, if our caretakers make any errors during that before-memory time, even if unintentional, we have no way of knowing.

I have no way of knowing what happened during my first few years, if anything. All I have is the feeling that remains.

–

Envision I'm a baby of between six months and a year old. I'm sitting on a floor in a white-walled room. A man stands before me. Beside me is a thing people sit on.

I recognize the man. He's somehow connected to the woman who feeds and dresses me. I don't have a name for him or her or the chair because I'm so young. But I know the man and woman are different from the chair. They're like me. They move and make noise. What they do determines how I feel: happy, scared, sad or any variety of other emotions for which I have no names.

I rely on people's eyes for clues about whether they'll be mean or nice to me. That's why I'm waiting for the man to look at me. I want an idea of what he'll do. The fact he hasn't looked at me yet makes me anxious because it's unusual. I've noticed when the woman walks in, she looks at me immediately. Then she smiles and picks me up. Sometimes, she jiggles me around while making faces and I feel warm inside and laugh.

After studying the room, the man lowers his eyes toward me. They reach my head, and without stopping, move down my face and body, and then slide sideways to the chair.

Something happened, though I don't know what. His eyes passed mine with no pause or smile or interest. He looks at the chair the same way.

If he's important to me somehow, he must know what's what. If he treats me like a chair, I must be like a chair. A *thing*, no worse, no better.

The Great Exploration

The boat,
made of a Bazooka
bubble gum wrapper,
floats
in front of me
down the creek
when I am four.

Though empty
of its pink cargo,
I know where
the folded prize
still hides,
snugged in the
U-shaped hull.

My eyes follow
the red, blue, white
as the ship pitches
in the rapids flowing
around my toes,

past sharp blades
of grass and whippish
willow sticks
dropped from trees
above.

I follow, mossy toes
submerged in cool mud,
my soul
as clean.

My hand reaches
for the sloop, for the
treasure inside, the joke
I don't know.

When I was about three and people asked my age, I'd concentrate hard to hold up only three fingers. I could tell by their amused smiles they thought I was having trouble remembering my age. Instead, the challenge was in getting my thumb to clamp my pinky finger, leaving the other three upright. I persisted until mastering the feat, just as I persevered at learning to tie my shoes. Whenever faced with a challenge, I felt both determined and strong because my older sisters made me so. And I was special to my dad, a guy who put on his shorts and ran somewhere every day, only to return sweaty and smelling icky, like spoiled milk. When not running around or at work, he fixed things around the house.

The way I knew I was special to him was because even though I was a third girl, and therefore no big deal, my dad called me *Sugar*.

Use of the nickname thrilled me for three reasons. The moniker was so much better than my real name, which I didn't hate, but didn't like either. And my dad called Mom *Sugar* too. He clearly loved her, judging by how he hugged and kissed her, so by default, anyone else on whom he bestowed the endearment had membership in the Cherished Members Club. Best of all, the nickname was the same word as my favorite ingredient. I loved anything containing sugar, whether birthday cake, candy canes or those orange Circus Peanuts in the crinkly plastic bag that hung on a hook by checkout lines at Kmart and that I'd successfully convince Mom to buy. I especially loved those sand-wich cookies with one vanilla wafer and one chocolate, a circle of stiff white icing lodged between them, three desserts in one.

During that time, we lived in Mom's mother's house. Grandma Edith had moved into a nearby condo with her youngest daughter, Mary, my aunt with Down Syndrome. Grandma Edith's house sat on an acre of land, a vast kingdom my sisters and I roamed every day. Even when rain poured, we donned our matching, shiny striped raincoats and hats that tied under our chins and went outside to stomp in puddles and look for worms. And in winter we wore mittens, often mismatched.

Our territory featured weeping willows with long stringy branches that dripped to the ground. If I closed my eyes and slowly walked through them, the way they brushed my cheeks and draped over my head felt creepy and shivery as the web made by the spider that scared Miss Muffet, a character I disdained even then for being a coward. Whereas my sisters and I weren't scared of anything. We caught spiders poisonous enough to kill us with one bite. But we always released our prisoners from their glass jars before going in for dinner. You don't kill things you find outdoors because that's where they're supposed to live. Even if I found them inside, I caught and tossed them out because mashing spiders made me feel sad.

Our land also featured a creek my sisters and I waded through while looking for tadpoles. The mud felt beautifully cool and squishy between my toes, like the liquid soap Mom used to wash dishes. The sun on the water sparkled with the brilliance of the stone in her wedding ring. The grass grew long and bendy and tickled when touching my neck. Whenever I found a Bazooka bubble gum wrapper, I'd take it to my oldest sister, who was old enough to read me the joke. They were never that funny, but I liked the little cartoon pictures.

I didn't go in the garage much because there was nothing fun inside. But sometimes I wandered in while my dad worked on the car. On those occasions, he worked in near-darkness by the light of a bulb hooked inside the open hood. Glowing a nice, daisy yellow, the light shone on my dad and his greasy old shirt. When I climbed up on the fender to see the car's guts, he'd say, *Get down from there, Sugar*, but in a nice way.

Not long after that, though, he stopped calling me *Sugar*. I didn't notice at first because I was too busy learning to color within the lines or jump across a swampy ditch. But then he called Mom *Sugar*, and I remembered he used to call me that.

I didn't know why Dad stopped using the nickname, only that he did. Without an official explanation, I searched for one. Maybe he thought I was too grown-up for that kind of pet name. But if that was true, he wouldn't call Mom *Sugar*, because she was old. Maybe dads just liked their kids for a while, then not so much. Or maybe he realized what I'd long suspected: that I wasn't really special. Just another kid, another girl. Whatever the reason, the loss of status made me feel sad.

Fortunately, I knew my sisters loved me a lot, and I loved them. While watching TV, they let me sit on the couch between them. With our legs touching, I felt like the frosting in a cookie sandwich.

—

Years later when my kids were in middle and high school, Mom came to visit as she did every year. I took her to Santa Cruz where we could walk along the ocean. During lunch at an outdoor cafe, we talked about a subject that prompted my memory and led me to say, "He used to call me *Sugar*, then he stopped."

"What do you mean?" she said.

"Well, just that he used to say things like, 'Hey Sugar, get down from there.' Then he didn't use that word. And he used to hug and kiss us, then that kind of stopped too."

Mom's brown eyes floated toward the sky. Quiet for a long moment, she finished chewing, then wiped her mouth with a napkin and said, "You know, when you girls were small, Dad told me about an article he'd read. About incest." She made a face of revulsion at the mention of the topic. "He and I, we were so square. We'd never even heard of that before. He was so shocked and disturbed anyone could do such a thing to a child. I'll bet that's why he stopped that. He didn't want you girls to feel uncomfortable."

"Well, okay, but it's not like we knew about incest either, right?" I said. "So how would we know to feel uncomfortable, especially if he wasn't doing anything inappropriate?"

She lifted her shoulder and dropped them, eyes filled with wonder, a common response whenever my sisters and I asked about dad's odd behavior.

"So he just got this idea in his head?" I said.

"I guess so."

"And he didn't consult you?"

She shook her head. "He usually doesn't, though. I don't know where he gets these ideas, but when he does, they stick in his head and you can't argue with him."

If he had consulted Mom, she would have told him we girls were too young to know about incest and that his actions toward us were those of a caring father and wouldn't be misconstrued. She would have told him to relax and continue to show us affection. Instead, he followed his lifelong pattern of forming an immovable opinion despite solid arguments to the contrary, a habit Mom found frustrating.

I tell him, but he never listens!

Deciding to err on the side of caution, he unilaterally and forevermore stopped employing any words or actions we girls might misinterpret as sexual in nature. Gone were normal fatherly hugs and kisses. Gone were endearments like *Sugar*. From then on, every conversation, gesture, letter and correspondence became stiff and formal, as though we kids were distant acquaintances of whom he had little knowledge. At night when he came to deliver a dutiful goodnight kiss, he'd land his hands on the pillow beside my head hard enough to make the mattress rock. Then he'd smack a kiss on my forehead before immediately pushing back to a stand and leaving. When I got older, if I did a good job during a band recital or other performance, he'd pat me on the back a few times, sometimes hard enough to knock me off balance.

As I watched Mom take another bite of sandwich, I marveled at how a loving dad could decide the only correct course of action would be to drop all loving gestures toward his kids. I placed the question in a box of inquiries which, if answered, might explain why I didn't feel close to my dad. A mystery that seemed increasingly important to solve.

A Gentle Hand

Much is said
when a gentle hand
is laid upon a
small head.

Our house in La Grange, IL, had shelves on either side of the kitchen sink where my mom displayed her bone china teacups and matching saucers. Made of porcelain so fine you could see through the glazed material, each cup had a slightly different shape and a unique design. The delicate painting of a Roman villa decorated a cup of sea green and white. Another had gold around the rim, a lovely contrast to a deep red bouquet of flowers on the side. Still another featured a fantastically intricate Moroccan pattern threaded with gold and emerald. Possessing an active imagination and a penchant for nineteenth-century English literature, I liked to study the designs and envision myself in the painted scenes. Of walking through a pasture at twilight. Of listening to a songbird perched on a branch. Sipping from such a cup made me feel like a character in an Emily Brontë novel, a grand lady living in a manor house.

A few times a year, Mom would pay my sisters and me to buff her tarnished silver wedding tea service—coffeepot, teapot, creamer, sugar, tray—for a special function, like an afternoon gathering of lady friends. On those occasions, she'd indulge her artistic nature and set out the teacups on a lacy tablecloth with trays of home-baked goods, a spread that could easily rival any Martha Stewart photo shoot array. Mom also sewed, sang, and arranged and rearranged rooms to create an ideal aesthetic. Of all the arts, however, she'd grown up wanting to be a dancer. Though she took classes and performed in recitals, she felt too self-conscious about her slight pudginess to dream big.

When I was about twelve, my mom began experiencing daily headaches that increased in intensity over the course of a few months. Subsequent tests showed a brain tumor, the same cancer that would eventually kill her decades later.

My dad, sisters and I took her to the hospital for surgery slated for the next morning. She smiled and said everything would be okay. Then we left. That night I asked Sue if Mom could die. Sue said yes. Though a brutal truth, I appreciated that she gave me a straight answer. The house remained quiet as we all kept to ourselves. I went to the kitchen. For a reason I don't recall, I reached for something on one of the shelves featuring my mom's teacup collection. A cup fell and shattered.

For a moment I stared at the wreckage without breathing. Despite having learned at a young age not to cry—*Quit your crying!* my dad would say. *Crying doesn't solve anything!*—I wailed. I felt like the breakage was a sign Mom was going to die. Maybe if I could save the cup, I could save her. Through bleary eyes, I gathered as many pieces as I could and set them on the kitchen table. I ran downstairs to my dad's basement workroom for glue. Running back upstairs, I sat down, wiped my nose, and with shaking hands, began gluing. The task focused my mind and made me feel better.

Using salt and pepper shakers to prop up the drying pieces, I reached a point where I had to let them dry completely before adding more. I went up to my room to read.

When I came down, I stared at the empty kitchen table. The teacup, all remaining pieces and the bottle of glue had vanished. I could hear someone downstairs in the workroom. I ran down and found Dad.

"What happened to the teacup?" I said.

"It was broken," he said.

"I could have fixed it!"

"Naw."

Crying again, I ran up to my room and lay in the dark.

The pieces, the bottle of glue, the props for drying: all indicated someone was working on a project. Considering Dad undertook fix-it jobs every day, he knew what an unfinished job looked like. Why did he throw away the materials without checking to see who started the task or why? Why this moment of illogical behavior when he was normally so practical? Not to mention methodical and dependable, especially regarding fatherly duties. He supported us financially. He came to band recitals and took us to the pool. So what if he never sought us out for the sake of being with us? So what if he didn't have the time to find out what we liked and how we felt? He was a real dad, unlike the fake dads on TV. Like Andy Taylor, the kind-hearted sheriff of the *Andy Griffith Show*, who'd take his son fishing and place a gentle hand on the boy's head. And Fred MacMurray on the TV sitcom *My Three Sons*, who'd walk into one of his son's rooms and ask what was wrong. Real fathers weren't like that. Real fathers went to work, came home, ate dinner and went to sleep. On the weekends they did things around the house.

Around, always around, but never with us kids. Never just sitting to have a conversation. Never asking us to go for a walk to find out who we were becoming. My mom called him an absentminded professor in a proud sort of way and claimed his intelligence eclipsed hers, whereas I thought, *Are you nuts?* Clearly she was smarter because she knew people. Their stories fascinated her. She could empathize with their struggles. She could figure out what was really going on, despite what went unsaid. Whereas my dad seemed incapable of any of those things. Though book smart, he had no clue about people.

Up in my room, I never once thought Dad might knock on my door to see why I'd gotten upset. He'd never done that before and never would. Just as I knew he'd never slip his arm around me or hug me warmly.

As I stared at the ceiling, so scared Mom might die, the even more terrifying thought came.

If she did, we'd be left with him.

Blind Mind

I think,

therefore,

you think

just like me.

Because ASD has *spectrum* in its title, we imagine a dial like the kind on an old-time radio. Those who register at the far left of the dial have high-support-needs autism. As the needle moves toward the right, the severity decreases. At the far right are ASD people who seem to get along fine and blend into a general population that includes a variety of more accepted types of neurodiversity, such as social anxiety disorder.

Rather than a dial, however, think of autism as a kitchen counter crowded with a dozen ingredients, including symptoms that have been mentioned before: hyperfocus, repetitive behaviors, difficulty empathizing and a tendency to meltdown when overwhelmed. Each person has a unique combination that might include more of one and less of another, which makes every ASD person completely different than the next.

Because I'm allistic, I haven't experienced the neurological condition, and therefore can't speak to what the biggest difficulty the challenge poses. I assume the answer is different for every autistic person. What I've read and have heard ASD people talk about most is how confused they feel when trying to communicate with allistic people.

When optimally developed, the human brain has a built-in decoder ring that over time and through thousands of interactions gains strength and accuracy. When we're around others, the decoder ring works furiously to interpret peoples' actions, tones, and expressions. When decoded, we have a fair shot at understanding people's behavior and their unspoken intent. If I ask how you are, and you frown and in a gruff voice say, *Fine*, my decoder ring tells me you're lying and are actually upset. Then I have a choice about how to react. I could say, *If you feel like talking about it, let me know.* Or I could remain silent, wear an expression that communicates I understand you're going through something, and I'll give you space.

In other words, engaging in the neurotypical communication system depends on the ability to interpret stated falsehoods. You can't necessarily go by what people say, but instead have to interpret their tone of voice and facial expressions, which is how you know a statement of *Fine!* might actually mean the opposite.

To a logical brain oriented toward literal interpretations, that unstated rule makes no sense and must feel exceedingly unfair, not to mention frustrating.

To understand the degree of that fundamental disadvantage in navigating a complex social code, consider that to survive we humans rely on two things: the ability to read faces and body language; and the skill of perspective taking, or Theory of Mind (ToM).

The ability to read faces and body language seems an obvious advantage in terms of survival. We take in information through our eyes, ears, fingers, tongues, noses and skin, after which the decoder works its interpretative magic to help us react optimally. We use that system to keep us safe physically, socially and emotionally.

Herman looks upset today, so I'll wait to request a raise.

That hulking guy looks like he wants to punch me. I'm leaving!

Charlene looks so happy when she gazes at me. I think she loves me in return.

Now imagine the challenge for ASD people who might experience such sensory input but be unable to accurately interpret it, a situation exacerbated by an unrestricted flow of sensory input that can lead to overload. Then consider some ASD people have the even more daunting symptom of *prosopragnosia*, known as *face blindness,* where the brain can't recognize faces. Or that some people on the spectrum lack an *affect*, which is the outward expression of an emotional state. As such, they might stare at others with an apparently emotionless expression known as a *flat affect,* which neurotypical people find creepy.

The second skill humans rely on is ToM, which goes like this: not only do I know I possess certain knowledge, feelings, beliefs and intentions, but I know you have your own, which is why you don't think exactly like me. Also, I use ToM to understand your behavior and make predictions about how you'll react. The more interactions I develop by playing with others, having relationships with parents and other kids, listening to stories, and taking part in social situations, the greater my ability to predict human behavior. And best of all, the better I understand others, the better I know myself.

Researchers believe the greatest spurt of ToM growth is between ages three and five. Delayed or truncated development can hinder the development of perspective-taking, which in turn can hinder the opportunity to show empathy. If someone says her cat died, allistic people will tend to draw on a similar memory of loss to access the feeling of that hurt, which allows them to empathize with the person. But if the listener doesn't know the social expectation of acknowledging the woman's loss, has never experienced the same kind of loss, and is oriented toward logic, moving on to another topic makes the most sense. Yet if the listener brings up a new subject, the woman gets upset.

If people lack a developed ToM, they might also assume what they think is what other people think. Imagine the frustration that can occur when people choose options you know are illogical. Or worse, they make those suboptimal decisions based on seemingly irrelevant factors, like accommodating others, when your solution is obviously so much more efficient. Why insist on keeping two people employed when the two jobs could be combined into one, a solution that costs less money?

The neurotypical use of imprecise language can cause further social confusion. If people are stressed about the amount of work they have to do, why not say that? Why use nonsensical terms like *I'm going bananas,* which makes no sense? And why do those same people laugh at those who point out the idiocy of the statement?

After learning about ToM, I revisited the broken teacup incident with the intention of putting myself in Dad's shoes, as best I could.

He clearly would have been as upset about my mom's upcoming surgery as my sisters and me yet might have lacked the self-awareness to acknowledge his emotional state, a blindness that became more evident over the years. When he found my messy project on the table, he may have grown furious at what he interpreted as an obviously thoughtless and disrespectful act committed during an already stressful time. I envision him grabbing the trash can from under the sink, and with bared teeth, sweeping the shards into the trash with one fast, violent stroke of his arm.

If my dad had possessed a properly working communication system, he still might have been upset and yelled for the perpetrator to present herself and explain the mess. I would have told him about breaking the cup and trying to glue the pieces together.

He might have pointed out the item was beyond repair. But I would have pleaded with him to let me try. The look on my face, along with my tone of voice, gestures and body posture, would have strongly conveyed my worry, enough to make him realize I was terrified Mom would die. Then he would have pulled me to him and comforted me.

I have no doubt if his decoder ring had been functioning properly, that's how the situation would have been resolved, simply because he was such a good man who tried his best every day.

But his decoder ring didn't work. None of us knew that. Nor did we know what effect his neurological difference would have on us.

Not for a long time.

Coffee shop

You put your hand on the cross
bar of the door, ready to leave
the coffee bar.

It's raining.

It was raining earlier when
you parked and got
out,

a moment where the world
seemed dusted in gray.

Metal, lights, the sun, all
done under.

But the coffee house
glows, and music
rivers

with mood and you smile
and work, and after a time
rise, taking the shine
with you

until your hand
lands
on the chill
of that cross bar

your skin
again cast
in gray, and you
think,

you *know,*
what you didn't
before
the artificial light
the recorded music

alone

and you push out
into the rain.

When I was eleven, my mom went to my parent-teacher conference to get an update about how I was doing. An average student, I obeyed the rules and mostly kept quiet. I enjoyed gym and music. While I didn't expect a glowing report, I didn't expect my mom's reaction either.

She sat me down at the kitchen table. She looked at me with concern and suspicion. Then said, "You're too good. That's what the teacher said."

"Too good how?" I said.

"Too well-behaved!"

"But, I mean ... What do you mean?"

"You're too quiet, for one."

"So I should start blabbing?"

"No, it's just ..." She *humphs* a little as she did when frustrated by my many questions. "It's good to be polite, but not perfect."

"I'm not perfect."

"But that's what the teacher said."

"Well, I can't help what she said."

Apparently unconvinced, Mom stared at me as though trying to figure out what mischief I might be hiding beneath my innocent appearance and behavior.

Exasperated, I said, "Are you saying I'm in trouble for being too good?"

"It's just ... It's okay to act out sometimes."

Now it was my turn to stare at my mom with skepticism because any kid with even average intelligence can smell a parental trap from miles away, and *it's okay to act out sometimes* is one of them. If I stepped off the straight and narrow, she'd *raise her voice* at me—adult-speak for *yell*—and say, *Wait until your father gets home!*

Rather than rile her more, I aimed for a look of shared torment and shrugged, as in, *You know teachers. Sometimes they're just crazy.*

Mom still seemed dubious. Eyes overflowing with concern that her *too good* daughter might be the mastermind of a criminal ring, she mentioned a few other things from her meeting, then let me go.

Rather than forget the comment, however, Mom raised the subject many times throughout my life. Maybe she held out hope for a juicy confession. Or maybe she felt if she reminded me enough, I'd have an epiphany that might solve a mystery she found unsettling.

She turned out to be right. The teacher's comment did point to a puzzle, one I unfortunately wouldn't solve until after she died.

In fact, her death gave me the key to understanding.

Rain on Leaves

The white fish eggs
of rain upon leaves—made greener
by the milky sky—
disappear
as I walk by, into
perfect clarity.

The teacher was right that I didn't talk much except to my sisters and a small group of friends. In large groups, I enjoyed listening and watching without the pressure to talk or entertain anyone. At home, I didn't talk to my dad other than normal dinner-table chat. I didn't have an emotional connection to him, a term that wouldn't be commonly used for another thirty years. Nor did I gab with my mom much, partly because I was the third kid. When I arrived, she was too busy running after two toddlers under the age of four to spend time alone with me. Not to mention in the 1960s, the parents' job consisted of keeping their kids safe, clothed and fed, whereas fostering their emotional development through *quality time* was a figment of the future's imagination.

Mom stayed extra busy trying to deal with my middle sister's behavior. Sue had a hard time sitting still, concentrating, staying organized and thinking before she acted. The diagnosis of ADHD didn't yet exist, so she grew up thinking she was a bad kid. She endured the criticism of my parents and most adults, who shook their finger at her and more or less told her she was lazy, disorganized and impertinent. Given Sue tried hard to do better, she was angry and confused that adults couldn't see her efforts.

Despite the fact Sue struggled more than I did, she was better than me in every way. She was unafraid to speak her mind. She was funny as hell. She excelled in all of her classes and played everything competitively: board games, her high school badminton team matches, our casual backyard croquet sessions.

And whereas I'd hound her to pay me back, she'd generously loan me funds and forget I owed her. An excellent baker, she instinctively learned chemistry from making those delicious sweets I mentioned earlier. And best of all, she befriended anyone who needed support, her empathy far beyond my own, even when young.

Yet without a formal diagnosis that could explain her challenge and inspire empathy from others, her self-esteem got squashed. Her condition led to frequent crises of lost homework, misplaced clothes and late arrivals. Whereas Mom tried to be understanding, Dad couldn't fathom why Sue didn't exhibit the same discipline he modeled. He seemed to assume she acted badly on purpose. The constant attention to her errors only exacerbated Sue's angst, made worse by huge undulations in her hormone levels that led to wild mood swings. Nor would Sue's naturally open personality allow her to hide her emotions. Unlike my mom, Sue talked about her feelings and had the chutzpah to tell bullies and unkind adults to go to hell.

Considering my crazy need to move, I most likely had—or have—ADHD. But early in my life, my brain must have latched onto organization as a means of survival. Like my oldest sister, I ran my busy life—sports, dance and as many other activities as I could fit in—like a CEO. I demanded no time from my parents. I saved and used my own money to buy things. I did what I said I'd do. At some point Mom began what would become a regular refrain she'd speak in a tone both certain and relieved. *I know I never have to worry about you.*

Every time she said that, I heard, *If you could please avoid doing anything to make me anxious, I'd be very grateful.*

To honor that unstated request, I avoided telling her anything and learned to appear fine, as in unruffled, without problems and more or less always on top of things. She seemed to appreciate the arrangement. In turn, I appreciated the clothes she sewed for me and birthday parties she threw for me and the sixty dollars—a huge sum—she convinced Dad to give me one Christmas to pay for dance lessons at the Chicago ballet studio my neighbor attended.

The cost of this don't-show-don't-tell policy only reared its head when Mom and I were alone, which wasn't often. When I fell out of a tree and was admitted to the hospital for observation of possible internal bleeding, she came to visit, but I didn't say much. I could see the sadness in her slumped shoulders as she left. But not only did I not feel guilty, I remember feeling the brutal, kid-true sentiment of *Good. You didn't want me to need you. Now I don't. How does that feel?* The same thing happened when she treated me to lunch after I got my driver's license on my sixteenth birthday. Again, I didn't say much, and again witnessed her frustration and disappointment that what she'd wanted to be special was not. But what did she expect? You either want to share in someone's life, which includes the low points, or you don't. You can't just scoop up the good moments.

I now look back and am sorry for the pain my repeated rebuffs must have caused Mom. Over the years, I came to learn my behavior was a symptom of my resentment at being disinvited to share the tenderest parts of me.

Of not being able to tell her—

I was so mad when Jeanne made fun of me in front my friends and I couldn't think of anything to say. Why would somebody do that, be so mean?

I had a dream I killed all of you and it made me so scared. Do you think I'm crazy and could actually do something like that? Because you know how I sleep walk. Do you think I could hurt somebody when I'm sleep walking?

What do you think happened to her, that lady, the one in the apartment next to ours, the one whose husband used to throw her against the walls?

Why doesn't Dad do anything with us?

Never feeling I had the freedom to speak about difficult things, my mouth lost the ability to put the right words together, much less deliver them. By adolescence, even if given an opportunity to express myself, I had no capacity for talking about what mattered.

While family dynamics played a role, the culture in which I'd been reared and the social habits passed down through my lineage added to my emotional muteness. As a suburban Chicago kid, I proudly thought of myself as a true American, meaning not a purebred anything, but instead a mutt of Welsh, Irish, Czechoslovakian, and a handful of other European and Eastern European strains. I went to school with kids of Irish, Polish, Slovakian, Lithuanian and Russian descent; cultures of cold climates and equally harsh *Quit your whining or I'll give you what for!* parental styles.

I have no idea who my dad's ancestors were or how or when they came to America other than that they arrived as immigrants looking for a better life. Left to my imagination, I picture a fairly impoverished European woman in the late 1890s who muscles her way through the crowd on the deck of a ship to catch a glimpse of Ellis Island with New York City in the background. She's thin and big-boned. A few strands of dark-but-graying hair blow about a face wearing the hardened public expression of *I will endure.* Yet inside, she's exhausted, worried about money, unclear about how she'll get along without knowing the language, fearful her husband might not be waiting, and very depressed she may never see her mother or other family members again.

Add to that a baby lodged on one hip while her free hand holds that of a toddler as two more children hang onto the hem of her coat. And so this little island of five descends the boat ramp and walks toward the processing building. When the woman gets to the window and speaks her name, the clerk stares at her, and with no attempt to clarify the surname, declares the woman will now be *Podhorn* spoken in a New York accent as clunky as the new spelling. The woman, upon hearing her surname demolished, is too tired to argue, and besides, the pronunciation is close enough. She just shrugs.

That shrug strikes to the heart of the matter. She, like the woman behind her, who will be crowned *McQueer*, and the man behind her, forever deemed *Putz*, and every person down the line, are from countries and generations in which once you're born, you work and then you die. During that life, you talk to each other but never really communicate. The Podhorns, the McQueers, the Putzes, all of them work their respective blue-collar jobs until the whistle blows, and when it does, they go home, end of story. You're hungry? Eat. You're tired? Sleep. You're in pain? Live with it. If you're like Dad's dad, who died when I was little, and you want your wife, Margaret, to make your favorite dessert, layered red and green Jell-O with the smear of cream cheese separating the two, you tell her.

Talking is for giving directions, not sharing emotions.

But that doesn't seem fair, a kid says.

Too bad. Life isn't fair. Now go do as I told you or I'll give you what-for.

Aren't you worried about forcing me toward an intrinsic lack of confidence that'll lead to an overt exhibition of hostility that could one day warp my happiness?

What? Don't give me that. Go to bed.

Words. Basic words. Words for communicating the basics. I'm here. You're there. You will. I won't. Go now. Shut up. Be quiet. Quit your crying. Vocabularies for those too busy, too tired, too uptight, too unused to talking about tender internal lovelies.

Shoved out of their home countries by poverty or war or persecution, those relatives of yore threw their meager collection of verbal tools into a burlap sack, cinched the neck, went to the new country and handed the bundle to their kids. Who handed the bag to their kids. Who handed it to their kids, until finally the mildewed sack comes to you.

You open the pack, dump the load and start making piles. One group contains the prepositions, pronouns and acceptable interjections you need for immediate use. *He, she, and, or, oh my!* Then you save a pile of common commands, politenesses and necessary remonstrations: *Come here, Please, Thank you, Get your hands off me!* And then you toss the antiquated phrases of *I won't settle for less than two oxen,* and *What a gay time we had!,* and *Groovy.*

Then you're suddenly out of material. Thinking you made a mistake, you sift through everything again for the combination of letters and words to match the sharp *thingamabob* swording around inside your head and the *whatchamacallit* flaming your gut, not to mention the *whatsis* making your heart squeeze through impossibly small places like The Blob, a squishy, unimaginatively named movie monster that slithers through doorways. But the words you're looking for—precise, dire—aren't there. Your descendants may have felt like you, but they never said so, and so bequeathed you nothing.

The more you experience, the more your inability to describe those dark feelings—of humiliation, grief, fear, hate—pushes hard against your tight lips. The pressure grows with every *I'm fine* spoken to cover an *I'm not fine* truth. Until finally the bolts of that Fort Knox strain, threatening to blow open and release a *barbaric yawp* forceful enough to destroy the world.

By thirteen, besides dealing with the hormonal changes of adolescence, I had a mind that wanted to know the why of everything and sucked down information of all kinds, even that which terrified me. Worries, angers, confusions, fears, all pushing in and packing together like so many scary clowns in a tiny clown car. They had no way to escape, except occasionally when I'd talk to my sisters about a worry I determined didn't sound too crazy. Angsts I knew would give my mother a heart attack if I told her and that my dad had no capacity or interest in understanding.

More and more until I felt my head would explode from passions my mouth refused to speak (insert exploding head emoji).

an afternoon of

autumn

nothing of autumn present

but the feel

a breeze, warm,

rolling the leaves

like surf

the roar, gentle,

the curl sudden,
strong

of

when I could

have—

Tight-Lipped Girl Salvation Strategy #1

I'm thirteen and sitting at my desk in my eighth-grade classroom waiting for the end-of-school bell to ring. A January day, I'm wearing my winter coat. My other thirty classmates are drawing, staring out the window or trying to finish homework. The teacher sits at her desk, correcting papers. She lifts a hand to adjust her glasses. She uses a pencil to write something.

The room is quiet.

I look down at the open pages of my book. And in the quiet, my eyes move over the words, reading them not fast, but

s
l
o
w
l
y

because I'm a slow reader, so slow I was placed in the you're-stupid group of readers in first grade. But by now, my subconscious knows I'm a smart reader and the speed with which I read is a barometer of a story's worthiness. The moment a book disappoints, I close it. If compelled to read for the purposes of homework, I skim as fast as possible.

But if I like a story, as I do *Jane Eyre*, the book I'm reading today, my hereditarily peasant, placidly pleasant mind chews the words, cud-like, while relishing the flavor, puzzling the meanings, and begging to be influenced. The nineteenth-century text insinuates an elegance into my thoughts, that *indeed*, upon being released from *this institution*, I'll *endeavor* to *traverse* the countryside *to my estate* where *I'll later dine*, very possibly on tuna noodle casserole from my *mother's Joy of Cooking* cookbook.

Books are for calming down and distracting the mind and allowing me to see how the characters struggle with difficulties similar to mine. Best of all, I start collecting those words that I'll eventually speak.

I write down those words in my new journal.

Tight-Lipped Girl Salvation Strategy #2

On my birthday a few months ago, my sister, Sue, gave me the journal with an inscription that encouraged me to write down my hopes and dreams. I started that very night.

Only years later do I find the courage to open the journal and read that first entry, as predictably desipient—*silly, trifling, foolish*—as one might imagine of an adolescent girl:

Oct. 22, '78
Today's my birthday, and what a birthday it's been!

After which the entry continues at nauseating length in said fashion.

And oh, woe is adult me, to see such nail-bitingly buoyant glee swimming around and around within that vast sea of exclamation marks. Though the term *OMG* is years in the future, I'll use it now,

OMG! Because the thing is—the thing *is*—there's something amidst the malarkey. An essence just beneath the overly sensitive inwardness of a thirteen-year-old kid. A substance beyond my obvious need at that time to shout challenges at a universal *them*, those nameless, faceless representatives of a humanity that will never read my journal, but if they did, would find I'm in control and not to be caught with my panties down or otherwise in a bunch. A quality that when you read the pages, you can see leaking out here and there, this stuff that can no longer be held, by which I mean, finally,

the words

for the feelings

previously inexpressible

and though I'm average and my feelings are predictable, I'm moving out from the shore, my shallows deepening. The progress of this profundity is literally visible in the places where my hand grinds the pen into the paper, cutting canyons that run ten-pages deep. Of thoughts not gleeful, not beautiful, not impressive, not that of a daughter, sister, Christian, Girl Scout, third kid, American child, suburban dweller. But rather that of a young, human life. Of thoughts vital and miraculous and finally hopeful, that one day they might be fully realized and found worthy, or maybe even remarkable. Me as no longer nice, polite, mouth-shut girl, but instead a yelling savage, one who's still years from being truly born, but is finally thinking, moving around, kicking, elbowing the boundaries, making myself known to me.

But at thirteen, I know nothing of what's happening, other than that there's an easing of internal pressure. Not enough to unwind my rubber-banded spirit, of which I'm still unaware, but enough to no longer feel like I'm choking.

Tight-Lipped Girl Salvation Strategy #3

The winter passes into spring. A few weeks after eighth-grade graduation, I get up early on a Saturday morning in June. Lilac-scented air wafts through my open bedroom windows. While dressing, I hear my dad in the bathroom, tapping his metal razor against the sink basin to knock off blobs of shaving cream and whiskers.

After a work schedule of up at six a.m. and home by six p.m. Monday through Friday, he usually sleeps late on weekends. But today he'll again make his commute by train to accompany me to my first ever ballet lesson. Finally, I get to attend Stone-Camryn, the prestigious studio where my neighbor takes class. The school is four blocks from where Dad works in The Loop, Chicago's downtown business district. I'm certain the studio, run by two old guys, will be where I'll make my name as a famous dancer.

Today's class is the first in a six-week summer course paid for with money I saved from mowing lawns and cleaning my neighbor's house along with the money my parents gave me at Christmas.

As I eat a bowl of Cheerios with two spoonfuls of sugar, Dad walks into the kitchen at a brisk pace while slipping his wallet into the back pocket of his trousers.

"You ready?" he says, continuing through to the back door.

I grab my bag, set my bowl in the sink and jog after him. I pass him and keep five steps ahead as we walk the six blocks to the train station where he shows me how to buy a round-trip ticket for $2.10.

On the double-decker train, Dad reads his *Chicago Tribune* while I watch the scenery pass, from that of my middle-class suburb to the older, more working-class neighborhoods closer to the city where smaller brick houses built close together line orderly streets. The train rocks and clicks, soon passing through the derelict inner-city neighborhoods where weeds sprout in empty lots and graffiti adorns boarded-up storefronts.

As soon as the doors open at Union Station, I jump off and move fast through the warm diesel fumes. I don't know where I'm going, yet manage to keep the lead by occasionally turning to ask my dad, *This way?* Sometimes he nods. Sometimes he points in the direction we have to turn. I try to memorize the route, because soon I'll be making this five-day-a-week trip by myself.

Finally, Dad and I come to a street where a train screeches on the elevated tracks overhead. We come to a doorway lodged between a tavern and a dry cleaners. On the wall next to the narrow stairs leading up, a small bronze plaque weathered to green reads *Stone-Camryn.*

I leap up three stairs and turn, the distance between me and my dad calculated to discourage any goodbye kiss, not only because we're in public, but also, I'm so tightly wound, any remotely sentimental move on his part might cause me to accidentally karate-chop him.

"Well," he says, his mouth open, as though ready to continue. But then his eyebrows lift and he laughs a little. "I guess there's no need to say *have a good time.*"

Turning, I take the stairs two at a time and push through the second-floor doorway.

Girls are everywhere. They clog the narrow hall with their legs spread wide in splits. They lean on the reception desk, talking to the older girls who get free lessons in exchange for manning the phone, handling payments and demonstrating combinations in class.

I head into the dressing room, shaking from fear of what I now have to do, change clothes in front of others. My neighbor's warning rings in my ears. *Make sure not to wear your underwear. It looks so stupid.* That's because the elastic band squeezes a girl around her thighs and waist. Within minutes of class starting, the leotard invariably rides up, showing the panties through the tights. The error is more embarrassing if the underwear features bright orange flowers, a pattern to which I'm partial.

Plagued by an ultra-modest upbringing, yet determined not to look like a newbie, I face the wall, slip off my shoes and change so fast I'm a blur to myself. Sweating and panting, I put on my ballet shoes, then follow the other girls up the stairs to the wood-floored studio.

At the head of the stairs is a small seating area with a baby grand piano. At the other end of the long, narrow room are windows open to the sounds of cars and buses passing below. Mirrors cover the front of the room, while every available wall features a pair of horizontal wooden barres. The room smells of gas fumes and rosin, the yellowish chalk dancers rub on their shoes so they don't slip.

My neighbor also warned me not to talk *on the floor*, a phrase referring to this room. But girls whisper anyway. They quiet upon hearing slow, heavy footsteps coming up the stairs.

Mr. Camryn rises into view as he holds the handrail to pull his old body up the steps. He walks onto the floor, a clipboard under his arm. Short, round-shouldered and slightly rotund, he wears a dark green T-shirt, beige britches that end at his knees, white nylon knee socks and sky blue ballet shoes. Around his wrinkled neck hangs a pair of glasses on a metal chain.

I love him already.

A second pair of feet stomp up the stairs. A tiny middle-aged woman with black hair and a big frown dumps her black purse under the piano and settles herself on the bench.

Mr. Camryn puts on his bifocals, lifts his clipboard, and without raising his soft voice, takes roll.

"Susan?" he says.

"Here."

"Amy?"

"Here."

"Martha?"

"Ya."

Even my eyebrows go up. *Ya*, like I'm Swedish or something. But it's out now, so I just look at him—*What?*—and wait.

Mr. Camryn smiles a little. "'Ya,'" he says.

When he finishes, he tells us to turn our backs to the barre and hold on with either hand. I glance at other girls to see what he means, then do the same. He counts the rhythm for the Russian piano player and she pounds out a tune as he speaks the cues we then follow. As a group, we lift to the balls of our feet, arch our heads back, press our bellies out, then return to an upright position and lower to our feet. Again and again and again until he tells us to stand sideways to the barre, feet in first position to begin a new move. For the entire hour, he watches us. No one chitchats. No one stops moving. The piano shouts. The floor creaks. Feet land, sweat flows, breath washes in and out, a wild ocean of effort. With every repetition, my movements grow and extend, my fingertips reach farther, my chin lifts higher, my legs lengthen until I feel like moving art made of pounding heart. And best of all—*best of all!*—my jumpy goddamn mind is suddenly, miraculously, fabulously quiet and focused. I'm in the here, the now, and for the first time,

I
am
free.

Tight-Lipped Girl Salvation #4
(For When All Others Finally Fail)

None.

walking at an angle

I'm walking along, walking
a long city block
when real—
ity unfairly shifts
slightly, everyone
suddenly striding
at an angle, but
me

who remains upright, even
as all around, tight
Pisa bodies lean,
expressions inclined
toward nothing
aslant

yet the gap is visible,
almost, between where
their heads were and
where they are now,
between the here
and the recently

was, the curve
between *then* and *is*
an abrupt
sliver of
confounding
distance

between a finger dialing
a number, the ear
expecting
hello
and getting *line*
disconnected,
the person there
yesterday—*there!*—
yet now disappeared
or maybe
never was

of a corner
store, one day stocked—
milk, bananas—
and the next, butchered
with papered windows
a sign of
scribble reading
out of business

of lips
parting for *love*
now askew with
never really did

gaps of deviation
that sheer reality
to a *what the hell?*
shimmer of chilling air,
the temperature
awry with the shiver
of vertical existence while
surrounded by people,
people everywhere,
coats buttoned to the arteries,
hair jet-lining
sideways, shod feet
smacking the concrete, walking
all walking

at an angle

When my sisters and I were little, our parents made clear they expected us to go to college and choose practical degrees that could earn us a living. Dee chose speech pathology. Sue chose nursing. And then there was me, split between the two hyper-competitive, low-paying and impractical loves of dancing and writing.

By now, though, I knew dancing was a no-go. Not only did I lack a beautiful dance foot that created lovely arabesque lines, but I felt increasingly frustrated I couldn't publicly convey the passion I felt inside. That left journalism, the only obvious means of getting paid to write. With my mom's research and application help, I enrolled in the University of Missouri-Columbia, the best undergraduate journalism school in the country. The moment I got there, I joined the student newspaper and radio station and began learning how to chase down a story, a skill based on developing curiosity beyond the size of ego.

That year my spring break didn't overlap with that of my sisters, who went to the University of Illinois Urbana-Champaign, so I spent the break alone with my parents in New Jersey. One morning as my dad passed through the living room dressed in his running gear, he stopped long enough to ask if I'd like to go to dinner that Friday. Given that he often treated our family to dinner at a restaurant whenever we returned home, I said sure.

On the designated day, I asked Mom what time we'd leave for the restaurant.

"I'm not going," she said with a smile. "Dad's treating *you*."

"What?"

Looking quite pleased, she said, "He wants to take you out."

"Why?"

"I don't know!" She shrugged extravagantly while maintaining that secretive smile.

While happy to see her joy, I knew something wasn't right. Only once before had Dad taken me—just me—out to dinner. That had been when we lived in Chicago and he took me to the cafeteria where he worked, after which we went to see *Evita,* a gift for my birthday.

The second reason dinner alone with Dad seemed suspect was that he never chose activities based on *hanging out.* Even if I explained the concept to him—*that's when you go to be with people for no express purpose other than to share their company*—he would have looked at me like I was crazy. In his world, every moment should be dedicated to accomplishing something *useful.* You go to parties to fulfill your duty as a good neighbor, church member, employee, father, spouse. You travel to learn, not lounge around, and you don't return to the same location twice just because you like it. When you decide on a family activity, everyone is invited to enjoy the experience, whether bowling, skiing or going to dinner.

Regarding the last, his culinary adventures were driven by reading *Chicago Tribune* restaurant reviews of ethnic restaurants. We ate crispy Duck à l'Orange at a place in Chinatown before Chinese food became a favorite American cuisine. When I tried stuffed grapevine leaves at a restaurant in Greektown and readied to spit out my first mouthful, Mom pointed at me, and with narrowed eyes, growled, *Don't you dare.* And I stared at my soup in an Eastern European Jewish restaurant, wondering how anyone could think floating cream cheese in cold beet juice was a good idea.

Lastly, the fact Dad and I didn't do anything one-on-one had become our norm. By inviting me to dinner alone, however, he was breaking the rules of our unspoken system. Clearly, something was amiss.

Then I remembered one of Mom's favorite childhood stories. When she was a junior in college, her dad invited her to dinner. She dressed up. He chose a lovely restaurant. They ordered, ate and talked. Mom said that was the first time she felt her dad actually got to know her, not only as an adult, but as a person. And how lovely to spend time alone with a man she rarely saw due to his constant business travel. Mom had been looking forward to future outings, but only a month later, her dad died of a heart attack while playing golf.

Maybe the reason Dad asked me to dinner was because Mom had encouraged him to treat me to such an experience.

He chose a nice restaurant not far from where my parents lived. We had a lovely time. As expected, I didn't have to talk much since Dad came to the meal prepared with a list of subjects he'd read about in the newspaper. Though a slow, methodical talker, he recounted facts with such accuracy as to relay fascinating stories, whether in history, finance, the trajectory of unlikely entrepreneurs or the close escape of victims trapped by disaster, such as an earthquake. As he talked, his mind seemed to chew on the concepts until he'd look at me, and with almost childlike wonder, say, *Can you imagine that?*

Nothing he said during dinner, however, revealed or confirmed the reason for the outing. Maybe he really had added *foster a more adult relationship with Martha* to his to-do list. Whatever the case, we had such a pleasant time, I thought he might be willing to go to dinner again sometime. Couldn't hurt to ask.

While reading in the living room the next afternoon, I heard Dad come up the stairs. I stood and waited for him by the kitchen. As he took the last few steps, he glanced up at me, eyebrows lifted in surprise.

Smiling, I said, "Thanks for dinner last night, Dad. Maybe we could go again sometime."

With no expression on his face other than puzzlement, he said, "Why would we?"

He disappeared into the kitchen.

—

Have you ever been stung by a bee and the stinger gets stuck so the flaming tip continues to drill into you? That's how the memory still feels, of his eyes as he said, *Why would we?* A pale blue that looked at me with nothing more than slightly irritated surprise, as if an inanimate chair had broken the rules by talking. An expression that didn't seem to understand what his words implied: *Why would I intentionally spend more alone time with you?*

Looking back, Mom must have guilted him into trying the father-daughter experience, not realizing Dad might acquiesce, though only in a literal sense. Her father took her to dinner once. My dad took me out once.

That and maybe, in his mind, the relative shortness of my stay elevated me to the status of *guest*, which obligated him, as the duty-bound host, to treat me to dinner.

Whatever the case, my dad and I never did anything together again, just the two of us.

Part III
My Parents

one

white sheet hangs
over a line
the two sides
separate, yet
each billows
against and
folds into
the other
one

When I was a kid, I never questioned why my mom married my dad because they clearly loved and respected each other. But as a young adult, I began to wonder why Mom chose such a quirky guy. After she died, I got mad at her for the choice she made.

Ultimately I think her insecurities drove her into his arms, something that's so utterly human and universal. We think we're choosing someone, when instead, we can't resist the haven they offer us.

—

Above my sink hangs a framed image of a single green pear rendered in colored pencil. Layers and layers of color have been used, so that while the fruit appears mostly green, when you look closely, you see hints of periwinkle, fuchsia, pineapple and dozens more almost-hidden hues.

The pear rests toward the right side of the frame against a white background. Light streams from an illusory *somewhere*, making the fruit shine. The beam also creates a deep, bruised purple shadow on the opposite side. Every time my mom considered the work, she lamented bungling the shadow.

I didn't get it right.

And how metaphorical that a woman who ran from shadows should admit to never working through them. And how true, too, that while she shone light and joy on everyone around her, she didn't treat herself as kindly.

Always creative, Mom didn't actively take up drawing until her sixties. She tried, and cast aside, a variety of mediums. To her, watercolor felt loose and reckless. Oil painting seemed unforgiving. In contrast, colored pencil allowed her the freedom to be herself: quiet, slow, meticulous, a lion of precision. Her mind centered on non-threatening natural beauty, she could think about what colors would achieve the effect she wanted.

On a few rare occasions, I called when she was in the middle of her work. Rather than her bright, sunny, *Hello, Honey!*, she greeted me in a low tone, as though having just woken up. Then she told me about the color of the pencil in her hand. A sea green, but would that do the trick? As quiet music played in the background, she wondered aloud if laying down a little tangerine first might illuminate an area from within. I remained quiet. Suspended in that moment of artistic reverie, we shared what truly mattered, being together during the creation of something beautiful. In that moment, I met my mother for the first time. A shy, artistic kid with curly hair and freckles, *this* was the real Norma.

Until then I'd only met the Norma who wore an exhausting public coat of cheerfulness topped with a bright, sunny inclusiveness. An apparent extrovert, she'd strike up conversations while waiting in a grocery store line, which embarrassed me no end when I was young. She laughed often, read voraciously and wanted nothing more than to be a wife and mom. The middle of three girls, she proved to be a natural caregiver and fondly reminisced about playing with her girlhood dolls. At twelve, she got her real-life doll when Mary was born. *She was the cutest little baby*, Mom would say.

As a teacher for the blind, Mom cared for her students. Then she met Dad, married him six months later and cared for him.

Within three years she had three little girls, and she cared for us. As time moved on, she sang in the women's church choir. She planned our two-week road-trip vacations. She organized our Christmas open houses where people stopped by in their best clothes and ate from the many goodies spread across our dining room table clothed in lace and Christmas decorations. She took care of the bills. She schlepped my sisters and me to music, dance and art lessons. When we moved to the house in La Grange, she repapered the walls of my room until they were covered in bright yellow flowers.

Mom had a strong empathic tendency and a good imagination, both of which helped her slip into someone else's shoes to understand their challenges. If she sensed they were uncomfortable, she made them feel at ease. If she suspected they were sad, she encouraged them to tell their story. When I was eight, she could tell I was nervous about going to my first sleepover next door, a span of two driveways. She sewed a heart-shaped pocket to cover a small marker stain on my little summer pajamas. And the gesture worked. During the night, I glanced down at the red heart and no longer felt homesick.

When she went to choir practice on Wednesday nights, I didn't go to sleep. Maybe even then I sensed she was the emotional thread that bound our family together, and worried about what would happen if that invisible filament broke. I'd wait until I heard her push through the back door downstairs, then stomp snow off her feet in the mudroom. In the kitchen, there'd be her muffled greeting to Dad. Then her feet would walk up the stairs. The footsteps would go to Dee's room, then Sue's, and finally to mine. She'd sit on the edge of my bed and lean down. I'd wrap my arms around her neck. She'd give me a series of little kisses, and we'd remain there for a long moment in that cozy embrace, until she whispered in my ear, *I love you so much*. Then I'd release her, feeling so much better. I'd been worried while she was out. But she'd come home. She was safe and she loved me.

So much tenderness, yet that purple shadow.

—

She treated herself harshly for a myriad of reasons. The first is that we humans—and especially women—tend toward self-unkindness. That internal criticism doubles if our looks and body type don't match those of women featured in media. Though Mom always took care of her appearance, she never escaped the image of herself as that awkward, chubby kid. And like all of us, Mom was a victim of the culture in which she was reared.

Her grandparents were solidly middle- to upper-class people who immigrated to upstate New York from Wales around the turn of the century. Photos of them clearly advertise the uptight upbringing they endured. My great grandfather, William Jones, has a handlebar mustache rigid as the wavy hair subdued by oil. His firm stance and fitted suit proclaim the affluence of an incoming manager at a slate quarry. His wife matched his demeanor. In the photo of this straight-backed beauty, Margaret stares into the camera wearing a fine, plumed hat. A third photo shows their two-year-old daughter, Edith, with the dark eyes she'll pass to her daughter, Norma, then to me.

Though I never met my great grandmother, there's a good bet she also passed down the era's preferred parenting technique, that of gutting your children via politely-worded criticisms meant to instill doubt and so corral them into conformity.

And you have the money to spend on something like that?

True, you could *wear that.*

Is it possible you did something to deserve that outcome?

A knife thrust dressed as a kiss, after which a mother could cleanse herself by saying *I love you and only want what's best for you.* An abhorrent, psychologically-twisted approach that filled my sensitive mother with self-doubt and would one day work its ugly way through me to my kids.

Despite the strict social mores of Great Grandma Margaret's time, her daughter, my Grandma Edith, possessed a mischievous sense of humor and a rebellious spirit. She gave up a potential operatic singing career to elope with her first love, Norman, a Hollywood-handsome local boy of French-Canadian origin. They married the same year as my dad's parents back in Alton, IL. Since married couples weren't allowed at their colleges, Edith and Norman got kicked out of their respective institutions. Weeks later, the stock market crashed and among other jobs my grandpa held to survive, he worked in a butcher shop to get free meat. Before long, they had William, who died in infancy. Then they had four girls: three in a close clump like my sisters and I, then Mary twelve years later.

My grandparents' crazy-for-each-other relationship apparently included crazy-mad-at-each-other arguments. One of Mom's favorite stories took place in a small, rented apartment in Detroit. Her dad had uprooted the family from New York for a job that soon failed. Stressed, surrounded by little kids and far from family, my grandma lost her temper and pummeled her husband. Fed up, he smashed his fist on the kitchen table with enough force to crack my mom's dinner plate down the middle, formally separating the potatoes from the meat.

The family resettled in upstate New York. My grandfather's work as a salesman took him away for weeks, during which my grandma presided over the household with a firm grip. When my grandpa returned to claim his role as CEO, my grandmother resisted the takeover. To say I come from a long line of strong females is an understatement.

Then Mary was born. Eight years later, my grandfather died of a heart attack on a golf course. My grandma had a full-blown breakdown in which she went blind for a time.

Amidst the periodic turmoil wandered the tender, emotional soul of my mom. Born with the natural urge to share her emotions and compassion, her upbringing and culture taught her—like many of us—to lock any nasties in a box you then hide beneath a bubbly public persona that proclaims, *I'm fine; we're fine; it's all fine!*

Not the prettiest, nor the slimmest, nor the one with the dazzling wit, my mom, like every kid, learned to use whatever attribute she possessed to help her survive and remain safe. A natural caregiver, she became a peacemaker during tumultuous moments. If she couldn't make peace, she stepped back into the shadows and remained quiet. When the situation calmed, she crept out to offer encouragement and cheerfulness she may not have felt.

I loved this woman who, with eyes bright, told me stories of running through the woods with her friends and not going home until called for dinner. In the outdoors, away from parental and societal restrictions, she loosed her imagination and became a formidable crusader. A child during World War II, she and her friends would pretend to be parachutists who dropped behind enemy lines during a vicious battle, only to save the day by performing some glorious maneuver. That vision of a girl seeing herself as a true heroine—not simpering, not beautiful, but instead hugely courageous—has served as the foundation for every female protagonist I've created. Females not as they're portrayed in so many movies, as sidekicks to be killed, and so provide male leads with the motivation to succeed, but instead as the universe around which the story takes place.

She gave me the strength to reject playing second fiddle, and instead, take hold of the life I wanted to live. My mother: a dreamer, a laugher, a girl who grew into a woman whose joyfulness overcame her tarnished self-esteem. A woman who every day viewed the world through glasses tinted in shades of delight iridescent as the pear she'd one day draw in layer upon layer of brilliant colors.

The strategy allowed her to avoid her boogeymen:

her low self-esteem.

her strong caregiving urge that turned to enabling.

how her decision to marry Dad might impact us kids.

It just happened

The hell it did.
No, it did.
Happen.
Yes.
Just.
Just happened.
Just?
What?
Was it just?
It wasn't ... it just—
Happened. It?
You know—
I don't.
It. Well. *It.*
Just some *it*?
Not just—
—any *it*, but a just *it*?
No.
No what?
Not just.
It was not just?
No.

This *it* that happened?
Yes.
That just happened?
Well, *it*—
What *it*? *The* it?
Yes, yes!
An *it* that just happened, as in just now?
Not now, it just— It didn't just—
It didn't just happen?
No! It, it—
—happened by itself? Justly?
No.
No what?
No it didn't.
It—
It didn't just happen. It happened—
Now?
Awhile ago!
Out of the blue?
No!
Just nothing, then something?
No, no!
Nothing that became something, but not just nothing-to-some-
thing, boom?
No boom.
It wasn't just boom?
It wasn't.
It wasn't just?
It wasn't.
You.
Me?

You allowed.

Yes.

You allowed it.

I allowed it.

To happen.

To happen.

Nothing, then something, then something more times ten.

Yes.

Then it.

Just happened.

Just?

It happened.

This just thing.

This … un-just thing.

This *it*.

Yes.

Mom said when she met Dad, they knew within a few dates they were in love and would marry. Over the years, she often repeated how she couldn't believe such a handsome guy would be interested in her. Though she grew into a slender young woman with a fabulous smile despite a mouthful of crooked teeth—one of the few uninhibited things about her and that I've always admired—she couldn't dispel the image of herself as a freckled, frizzy-haired kid. Nor could she shake her unspoken fears, so that when the time to marry arrived, she chose the safest person she could find, Raymond E. Podhorn.

Without exaggeration, Dad could have been a Paul Newman stand-in, complete with blue eyes and the muscled physique he developed from a daily fitness regimen. Unlike celebrities, however, he was a good Catholic boy indoctrinated against adultery. Hyperfocused on his duty as a good husband, he treated other women with no more than the politeness he'd afford anyone. When he played the role of a military higher-up in our church's production of *South Pacific,* the script called for him to pat a nurse on the behind. Rather than embrace the character of a lusty man, Dad performed the action like a man ordered to slap a beehive.

Dad wrote Mom poems. He gave her flowers. He pulled out her chair and complimented her cooking. He thought she was marvelous.

The sheer wattage of the golden spotlight Dad shone on Mom must have dazzled her and made her feel like someone she'd never been before, a glamorous leading lady. I imagine the slightly dazed look in her eyes at having won the jackpot by gaining the attention of a man who checked every box:

handsome.

loyal.

a good provider.

safe.

someone who made her feel like a goddess.

someone who insisted she was better than she gave herself credit for.

So what if she, a Presbyterian, had to agree to rearing her kids as Catholic?

So what if her husband was a little quirky here and there?

For those many reasons, she repaid Dad with undying loyalty. Given the green light to indulge her natural caregiving tendencies, she became that brave parachutist who acted as Dad's shield. She smoothed over any awkward social moments. She distracted and calmed him if he got irrationally upset. She reminded us that while Dad didn't seem to understand us, he loved us.

She also enabled him to act badly by excusing his conduct. On those rare occasions he freaked out, she stepped back and shut up, then dealt with the aftermath. Because when something scary or disturbing happens, you don't risk your happiness and emotional and financial stability by contemplating the possibility there's something fundamentally wrong with your husband.

Something scary like when we adopted a dog from an animal shelter.

We'd had the dog for maybe a year when he pooped on the carpet. Just like the snow-rolling incident involving Sue, Dad interpreted the deed as a sign of canine disrespect. Most likely also fueled by stress he couldn't see, much less acknowledge, he narrowed his eyes and with bared teeth and that whip-fast strength, dragged the dog down to the basement and beat him as my sisters, Mom and I cried and yelled for him to stop. After that, the dog turned mean and growled at us.

The next summer my sisters and I went to visit my grandma, who'd moved back to upstate New York. Before my sisters and I returned home, Mom called. She solemnly told us the dog had lunged at the mailman. Fearing the dog might one day actually bite someone, she had the dog put to sleep, after which she cried all day. In truth, my sisters and I were relieved, because the dog scared us. What went unsaid, but that all four of us understood, was that we'd found Dad's behavior scary too. The viciousness. The inability to understand the dog had no ill intentions, but instead might have been sick, or maybe we hadn't let him out to do his business. We'd witnessed the dog turn mean. And we'd witnessed Dad.

Only later in life did Mom mention to my sisters and I how she sometimes wondered if Dad was a nut. Her tone would be that of a wife who simply wondered why he acted wacky sometimes. Again, this was before any substantive knowledge about autism, and again, this was Norma, peacemaker and steady-the-boat passenger.

That role of conciliator kept Mom forever between Dad and us girls. There she remained, a buffer of softness against Dad's rigidity. We knew if anything happened to her, Dad would feel duty bound to rear us with military precision, unaware of squashing us in the process. Hup-to, hup-to. Stay within the lines and no lip. Duty rules. If you get married, you stay married. If you have kids, you love them, emotion having nothing to do with anything. You send those kids to college so they can support themselves, just as you perform certain social functions because they're expected of you: Fourth of July picnics, your kids' band concerts, Christenings and graduations. And if the young fatherless son of a family friend needs some instruction on how to be a man, you invite that boy over to do manly things like hammering and nailing. You certainly don't notice that your youngest daughter watches in rage because you're spending time with a boy you don't know when you never spend time with her. And sometimes, amidst all of that drilling, sergeanting and dutying, you hear a forceful, yet soft voice by your side saying, *Now Ray, let's calm down.*

There stood Mom; not a referee, impartial to either side, but instead, Dad's protector, enabler, excuse, and cover.

If my people-pleasing mom had a normal relationship with a dad who'd been around, maybe she would have recognized something off in how we interacted with our dad. But she didn't. And because she grew up in an era when people didn't *talk things out*, she never had the words or practice necessary to discuss Dad's scary incidents with us, especially when those moment may have embarrassed or frightened her too. Then consider that in the 1970s, a father's only job was to support his wife and kids financially. Taking kids' feelings into account was considered hooey. They should appreciate what they get and do what they're told. Looking from the outside in, most of my friends' dads seemed like mine. They worked a lot and paid attention to family. By those metrics, Dad succeeded.

Lastly, there was no way for Mom to detect we had no emotional relationship with Dad, given his daily actions seemed to prove otherwise. Unlike her dad, our dad was always around. He regularly took us places. During the summer when he got home from work, he'd drive us to the pool where he'd swim laps and then throw us around in a way that made us shriek with delight. He ate dinner with us and told stories of being in the Army. He took us to church every week. He barbecued for us and took us skiing and laughed at the excitement on our faces as we opened Christmas presents.

He was a good man who lived a good life and, like any of us, did the best he could with what he had. If I'd told him we didn't have an emotional relationship, he wouldn't have understood. He'd done all he could, right?

Right.

—

I found a few articles about adults who were assessed and diagnosed with ASD and, as a result, experienced relief. After feeling out of place for most of their lives in how they act and respond socially, they're happy to learn the culprit is a neurological difference, one with a name, symptoms, coping strategies, research studies, and treatments for handling ancillary problems like ADHD and anxiety.

Sometimes I imagine sitting across from my dad the year before he died. I hold a microphone that connects to the headphones he wears, a system that allows him to hear. He's in his wheelchair, arms on the rests and his posture bent. He looks at me with his blue eyes, waiting.

I say, "Dad. You know how Brian and Sean are on the spectrum?"

He pauses, then nods.

"And you know there's a strong genetic component to autism. Do you think there's a chance it came through your side of the family?"

His bushy, white eyebrows rise, apparently surprised by the question. Then his logical brain gets to work. After a long pause, he says, "Well, according to the laws of genetics, that's certainly possible."

I say, "Do you think you have autism?"
He looks down for a long moment, then looks up at me, his eyes sharp with intelligence, and says, "I guess it's possible."

Unskinned

He's broken-finger bent,
the old man.

One look and you throb
for him, at how
he sits, on the edge
of a recliner not reclined,
not relaxed.

The hump of his back
forces him forward
and down—
his shoulders, his head—
the bulk of him gone.

His hands,
the fingers sausaged,
the joints bouldered,
hang between his legs,
while his eyes
beg, because,

blue-collar born, he does
not understand
the bonfiring of a body, a soul,
her soul.

She gazes at him,
from a body laid out,
tubed, pained, pilled,
reclining toward forever.

He leans the hurt
of him closer:

the cracked clavicle
that collapsed him, the
ankles that cave, the
ears that make his world
a silent film.

Only the bony
arches of his eye sockets,
keep his flesh from
rushing downward, leaving him
unskinned.

She's whispered her wish
for fire, her fear of cold,
black, wormy
mold
complete.

And he says to her,
says to his wife,

It would change
how I remember you.

Because bodies
he understands.

Bodies broken,
bloated, breathless.

Bodies danced till dawn
and knuckles sliced, salt
sprinkled in the wound.

Bodies sleek with preen
and cascading water.

Bodies covered
in bumps of shake, the
bones river-town reared
and later suburban housed
through years of work, bellies
caked on birthdays and
wined on anniversaries, blood
rushing on the river
that is making love.

Bodies
bruised
bound
radiated
twisted
sprained
their mass contorted
in torture
and joy.

Whereas ashes ...

They are something
that is nothing
without the hurt.

When Mom's cancer metastasized, her almost superhuman ability to look at the bright side dominated for about three years as she moved from one treatment to another, one experimental drug to the next. Even now I shake my head in admiration for such optimism, even when the drugs caused sickening or embarrassing side effects. I've long said I owe my mother everything for genetically bequeathing me her chronically happy body chemistry, one of the greatest gifts I've ever received.

Before she died, I went over my thoughts and experiences to make sure nothing had been left unsaid between us. I could think of nothing sadder than forever losing the opportunity to clarify misinterpretations or offer apologies. Long gone were the days of mean-spirited adolescence in which I rejected her for perceived neglect. While I still didn't share important internal thoughts, lest I worry her or invite those politely-worded criticisms, we existed on a comfortable level of love and appreciation. Though imperfect like the rest of us, Mom had been an ideal mother.

I had nothing left to tell her, which made me feel so good.

So sure.

—

In those three years during which Mom had a fairly good quality of life, my dad moved along with her as though no disease threatened her. You get married. Your wife gets cancer. You correct the problem as you would a clogged gutter.

But there's no fixing metastasized cancer. Instead, patients like Mom move from one experimental treatment to another in hopes of staving off death for as long as possible. But, eventually, the day comes when the doctors say, *There's nothing left to try.*

When the specialists made that pronouncement to my parents, Dad heard the words but didn't digest them. His reaction could have simply been due to denial, which is a common response, according to Sue, a hospice nurse. Yet for an unusually logical man, the gap in his understanding seemed monumental. He knew people die and that cancer is a common reason. Yet he didn't seem to believe those facts in Mom's case. If he felt physically fine and clearly wouldn't die anytime soon, that must be true for Mom too. If she wanted to stay alive, she should follow the program that worked for him, of exercising daily and eating healthfully, meaning lots of bran.

When she began to fail, my dad's symptoms of apparent autism became more pronounced. He didn't believe doctors' claims that there were no more treatment options, given he found articles on the internet about experimental drugs now in development elsewhere in the world. After listening to the advice of Mom's doctors and Sue, who acted as our family's medical guide and advocate, Dad appeared to agree with how to mitigate Mom's pain. Yet his rigidity in thinking caused him to act according to his theory that Mom brought this cancer on herself due to an insufficient fitness regimen and an inferior diet. Emotionally he often lacked empathy regarding her pain and fear. During chaotic moments, he'd have angry outbursts.

He'd encourage Mom to walk, despite tumors that made such movement excruciating. He'd get her situated in the rented hospital bed placed in the guest bedroom, then wander away for long periods to eat his dinner or check his investments, during which he couldn't hear her calls for help. Desperate, Mom would struggle with the cell phone to call Sue, who'd race over to deal with pain that had skyrocketed to a level of ten out of ten.

Mom needed twenty-four-hour care. Dad disagreed. He couldn't seem to understand such care would increase Mom's comfort and unburden my sisters, who acted as her primary care-givers by checking on her daily, organizing her pills, arranging medical equipment rentals and taking her to doctors' appoint-ments, all while working full-time and rearing families. Though he agreed to try a few home health aides, he inevitably dismissed them because he didn't like strangers hanging around his house. If you pay someone, they should be working every moment, not watching you go about your normal routine.

In the spring, I flew to the East Coast to accompany Mom and Dad to New York City for her doctors' last-ditch attempt to slow the cancer with a massive dose of radiation. Mom, Dad and I checked into a studio apartment sponsored by the hospital to house out-of-town families. That night as I curled up next to my mom, who whimpered with pain and the fear of dying, Dad ate his dinner. I thought seeing Mom in such distress would cause him to comfort her. When he didn't, I got up and told him he needed to go to her. He seemed confused but did as I asked. When he sat next to her, she wrapped her arms around him and sobbed. He patted her shoulder.

When the doctors and my sisters encouraged Mom to start hospice, Dad criticized her for *just giving up*, despite an abdomen swollen with tumors. After my visit the following September, when Mom almost died from severe dehydration, he began pushing liquids on her. During my visit in November, Mom asked me to set up a time for the funeral director to visit. She wanted her wish to be cremated put in writing and prepaid. She knew Dad wouldn't honor her verbal request because he didn't like the idea of cremation.

Despite Dad's dogged attempts, which kept Mom in torment for several more months, death won.

Mother

If I could I would deliver you
to Valhalla.

If I could

I would

at the moment your eyes
drifted just beyond
seeing me

ever again,

swaddle you in the finest gold-braid
pharmacology had to offer
the stitching impeccable:

—strong, enduring—

offering an embrace
in which you

fear nothing

anymore.

Then I would—

    —we all would, your clan—

  soldier you fast

     fast!

along a harbor road,
riding—

—thundering, yelling—

whooping!

life in our voices, and
     ferocity, too,

for you,

so deserving of lightning
movement, of crackling
heart.

All of us conveying
you with

speed

beneath tremendous
clouds

—banners snapping—

toward your ship
where we

draw up
lift you aboard
kiss your cheek

so still now.

All of us still
now,
in the wind.

And then I'd raise
my arm, and we, all

of us who carried you

—who carry you—

would roar with

joy

the piquancy stabbing,
the pain
that pure.

And I would untether your
forever shelter

to drift you on the lovely
currents, your face up

—open—

to all that's beautiful.

I would—

—I will—

my Warrior
      Queen.

When my sisters and I began to suspect Dad might have undiagnosed ASD, we found clues from our past that made the
theory eminently plausible. Even then, though, I still thought his
possible autism only affected him. He'd always been so *over there*,
I couldn't see the truth sneaking up on me. Though awkward,
well-intentioned and mostly harmless, Dad had the capacity to
decimate others emotionally, and would unintentionally do so
again, until finally displaying the impact of his suspected neurological condition on my sisters and me.

I should have guessed at that future reckoning based on his
response to nineteen-year-old me when I asked if he'd like to go
to dinner again sometime, just the two of us.

Why would we?

—

A second warning arrived during my mom's funeral.

A lifelong devout Catholic, my dad regularly donated to the
church's various causes. He went to Mass more than once a
week, attended confession and said nightly prayers, all based on
the belief that enduring life's torments would be rewarded with
eternal life in heaven where you'd be with the people you love
most.

Then during my mom's funeral, Dad asked my husband, an
atheist Jew, *Do you believe in the afterlife?*

When my husband later told me about the odd exchange, a shiver of heat ran through me as a revelation dawned. The incident solved a three-piece puzzle about why Dad had so desperately resisted my mother's death, then resented her for dying, after which he clung to life with every ounce of his being via exercise and his version of an ideal diet. Despite his decades of religious study and dedication, he doubted what he'd been told. Specifically, he doubted there would be an afterlife.

His keen intellect, which so voraciously absorbed books about history and the universe based on facts and proven laws of physics, now fought with his duty to believe in a magical existence after death. The logic won. He hadn't wanted Mom to die because he didn't think he'd see her again. He didn't want to die because that meant lights out for good.

—

A third and final warning occurred the night before my husband and I flew home from the funeral trip. I went to Dad's newly-quiet house to keep him company while he ate dinner. By now he was almost totally deaf. He'd never found hearing aids he liked and my sisters hadn't yet discovered the microphone system he'd use in the year before he died. Talking to him meant visually getting his attention and standing close enough he could read your lips. Rather than try to make conversation, I remained silent. If he wanted to talk, I'd listen.

He roamed the kitchen, heating up various liquid drink combinations and pouring mixed sauces on solid items like his own meatloaf infused with bran.

Then he looked at me and said, "When we were in New York City and Norma was crying, she was scared, right?"

For a moment, I couldn't parse his question. Not only had he jumped nine months back in time, but his question implied he still didn't quite understand what had happened that night in the hospital-sponsored apartment. Though apparently unable to feel her agony, her behavior must have struck him as odd enough to warrant more thought. His logical brain had chewed on the clues—how I told him to go comfort her and how Mom hugged him and cried—until he developed the theory she'd been afraid.

I paused for a long moment, for the first time seeing how deeply he didn't understand. I wanted to say, *Not just scared, Dad, but terrified.* Instead, I nodded.

"That's what I thought," he said.

He looked relieved to have solved the puzzle. But he never did accept that a disease killed her. Instead, he repeatedly expressed his belief that she'd given up, and if she'd just tried harder, she might still be alive.

And there you have it, I thought, a man talking smack about his dead wife, whom he'd loved and cherished for fifty-two years.

Part IV
Crisis

Truth

A full-length mirror
holds a figure, naked,
scar a clear white
in morning light.

Not long after Mom died, I felt strange in a not-good way. I knew the stages of grief, yet something seemed off about my version of the floaty, distracted mindset supposedly typical of new loss. I'd had the time and opportunity to say goodbye to Mom. I felt sure we'd parted on the best possible terms. I loved her and she loved me. We had many happy memories, especially of her visits to California. We visited wineries, went for walks and watched the ocean, of which she never tired.

But after her funeral, those memories began to intermingle with the many clues of Dad's possible ASD. The Polaroid brightness of my youth began to fade and distort. I already knew he and I had no real relationship, which was nothing more than fact. I still appreciated his many years of love and support.

Then I began to realize my mom and I had operated at a similar surface level as well. Her role as Dad's protector, when coupled with our unspoken agreement I wouldn't cause her any worry, meant our encounters had been the meeting of two public personas, hers and mine. But maybe that was how a lot of people felt about their parents, of loving them but never feeling able to tell them anything that matters. While plausible, some part of me remained dubious of that explanation.

The idea I'd emotionally shut out not one but both parents at an early age remained a distant and unfocused possibility until a month after Mom's funeral when I called Dee. I remember little except sitting on my couch, a bright floor lamp shining over my left shoulder.

"You know what's strange?" I said.

"What?" she said.

"I don't think Mom ever really knew me."

"What do you mean?"

But I couldn't explain, or at least not well. The closer I looked in the coming days, the clearer the answer became: I thought I'd hooked myself deeply into Mom's foundation, only to learn my handhold had been fictional. Dad and Mom had not been there to catch me emotionally, so I grabbed onto my sisters and held tight. Had I known that to be the case, I might have been all right. What startled me—woke me, shook me, slapped me around—was how oblivious I'd been to the truth: that I hadn't bonded with either parent, a critical step in helping kids develop a sense of self-worth.

What else had I missed? What else had I lied to myself about?

One moment I was a person who thought I understood what was what, only to realize I didn't know squat. The not knowing— not seeing, not suspecting—was what speared me. A natural observer who closely analyzed others, I now wore the dunce cap. I didn't care about the humiliation associated with such punishment. Instead, the disorientation upended me.

As a writer, I hate clichés, yet found myself suffocated by them. Where I'd been *standing on solid ground,* the earth now *crumbled beneath my feet.* By dying, my mother *set me free,* but also *yanked the rug out from under me.* The once smooth road *now grew dark and treacherous.* My mind swam amid the nightmare of trite phrases because I couldn't describe to anyone, much less myself, what it felt like to suddenly wake up, a bewildered Rumpelstiltskin, only to realize I'd been living under two delusions for not just awhile, but my entire life: the first, that my mom and I had a close relationship, and the second, that I'd always acted true to myself. If

I'd been pretending with my mom and myself, had I also done so with family and friends?

If I wasn't no-trouble-to-anyone Martha, who was I?

After that revelation, my voice sounded normal, my body felt normal and I looked normal. I went to work the next day and the next and planned this and that. But as the days passed, I felt increasingly confused and isolated.

—

If you have a more or less happy life, you feel you have no right to complain. Whatever happened to you is far better than the unspeakable ways in which others suffer. The world around me reflected that attitude of *Don't be a crybaby. Be grateful for what you've got.* So after noting the fact I'd internally blown up from the enormity of my self-delusion, I continued to move through my days, mouth shut about my epiphany and amazed by how my exceptionally normal external appearance hid the internal tornado of debris whirling inside. Up was down. True was false. Black was white. What I thought I'd had was gone.

I was forty-seven, and until that moment in my life, had always known my path and wondered why some people floundered. Didn't they understand if given a handful of acceptable routes, they should just choose one and drive forward? And what was all this mid-life crisis crap?

Now completely lost, I faced the brutal truth that despite my unconscious attempts to be Miss Perfect, I was not only hugely imperfect but totally screwed up.

What had gone wrong in an otherwise privileged life?

Something big. Something unseen. Something that might swallow me whole.

To shake,

be shaken,
made to finally forsake
sameness

swallowed into an early sea
—of see

after so much calm
so much being
a flag post, so

stuck

in the ground, everything moving
about it, wind, sun, thunder—
—storms, all of that
ferocity, yet
so unmoved

unaffected, at first
a lauded result, a pillar
so evidently

straight
tall

a monument to oneself
identifiable anywhere, the tip
above, looming,
do you see it?

Always in one
place, one plane, one direction-
less soul

so what becomes necessary is the earth
to roll, to coil, to

writhe!

to loosen what's been compacted, the stone
the grit, the dark matter
of reality, the illusion
of surety

breaking apart, crumbling, separating, sieving
the solidity, all that's left
a handful of loose rock

bare

Seven months after Mom died, I made my normal sojourn to the East Coast. I didn't want to stay with Dad, though I didn't know why other than that I had no practice at being alone with him for more than a few hours.

After arriving in Connecticut and settling in at Dee's house, I understood my obligation to visit Dad but felt nervous to do so. My sister told me to relax. Now that Mom was gone, Dad wasn't acting as unusual as he had been during her last year.

I wore shorts and a T-shirt and rode my sister's bike to his house. Now noon, he'd finished his exercise and moved around the kitchen fixing himself his various juices. I sat down and settled in to listen. I expected him to talk about the weather, finances, and topics he'd read about in the newspaper, after which I'd leave. Instead, he got to talking about how he and Mom had loved to travel.

Every four years or so he'd accompany her to California to visit me and my family. Though we had a guest bedroom, he insisted he and Mom stay in a hotel, claiming he didn't want to put us out. Yet Mom and I knew he simply preferred having his own space. After his morning of running and drinking his liquids, he and Mom would arrive at our house, ready to do something he found worthwhile, such as visit a museum. After a few days, he and Mom left to visit somewhere they'd never been.

As Dad reminisced, he mentioned how Mom came to visit me every year around my birthday. By his comments, I knew she hadn't told him what she'd told me: that she liked to visit without him. Rather than a short visit with us, she'd stay for about ten days. She'd get up and wander into the kitchen where we'd have a leisurely breakfast in our pajamas. Then whenever we were ready, we'd head out for the day on some adventure, which could be as simple as shopping for kids' clothes or going to a movie. Without Dad—without a schedule—we relaxed and had more fun.

As Dad moved around the kitchen that summer morning, he said every year he offered to accompany her. After a short visit with us, he and Mom could then do as they normally did and go somewhere they'd never been. Yet Mom had insisted the point of the trip was to come visit me.

At that point in the narrative, he looked at me, and with genuine puzzlement, said, "Why would she want to do that, just go to see you? I never understood that."

Why would
she want
to just go
see
you?
As in, *What's there to see?*

—

When freelancing for the *Chicago Tribune*, I interviewed a man in his suburban home for a feature article. Amidst our discussion leading to his accomplishments, he talked about his upbringing on the South Side of Chicago, a notoriously tough part of town. When he was a teen, he got into a fight with another boy. During the altercation, his opponent slipped a stiletto knife between his ribs.

Though decades beyond that moment, just the memory caused his eyes to open wide with surprise. He physically winced as though the blade had just entered. Though the wound had long since healed, the trauma remained. With pain in his eyes, he said, "In all the movies, they don't tell you that, how much it hurts."

So, too, when my dad spoke those words to me that summer day after my mom died. One moment he was my dad. The next he was the sea serpent who reared out of the depths, closed the distance between us and slipped the unwitting slight deep into the soft tissue of my being.

Dad was just being Dad. Blunt, literal, logical. What he'd meant was that he wanted the kind of trip he wanted. He found visiting relatives boring, especially since he didn't like to sit. But once he fulfilled his duty, he could visit somewhere new and have fun. He didn't understand what his statement implied, that I was not worth spending time with other than what was necessary to fulfill an obligation.

While the bluntness of that message hurt, what seared so deeply was the way he looked at me, with eyes brutal in their indifference. In a way that said:

I was neither interesting nor uninteresting.

I was nothing to think about.

I was just there.

Like a chair.

In that breathtaking moment, what was left of my world dissolved. For the first time, I stared with wonder and agony into the abyss of Dad's apparent disability. I hadn't known its depth, but now I did.

I'd never experienced a panic attack. But after leaving his house that day I had every symptom: shallow, quick breathing, blood pounding in my ears, a body that shook from the adrenaline of a psychological shock. I went back to my sister's house and spent the next two hours calling therapists on the list provided by my insurance company.

Because now I had to tell someone I'd been attacked by the sea serpent I'd always feared. That rather than rear up from the depths of a calm lake, the beast had disguised itself as a stooped hundred-and-forty-pound man. With one last, fast clawed snatch, he pulled me under.

Foundational Sheer

Because they built in earthquake
territory

they bolted
their square
wood frame to a
square concrete slab.

But then came a tear
of unexpected
strength, enough
to sheer the
bolts.

The frame and slab, they
used to be together,
but as you can see, they're not
anymore.

When reading novels, I love a mind-blowing turn of events. In real life, not so much.

I'd always thought I had a good self-esteem. I accomplished my goals, felt sure about what I loved to do and didn't take guff from anyone. Yet in the moment my dad implied I was a daughter, yes, but other than that, an obligation, I realized my self-esteem may have suffered as a result of being the child of a possibly ASD dad.

Then, like an aftershock more powerful than the original earthquake, I realized I had no self-esteem at all.

—

The best way to understand that concept is to think of yourself as Casper the Friendly Ghost from the cartoon. You're an invisible being who can see everything around you, but nobody can see you. What fun! You can watch people's actions and expressions with abandon. You can attempt to discern their relationships and detect their insecurities. You can listen to their tones and accents and the words and phrases they use, all while moving among them with freedom. People sense you're nearby, but you learn they're much more interested in themselves than anything else. If you get bored, you slip away. The only people who can see you are your sisters. And though you're nothing, they still like you, and you're glad for that.

Being invisible to almost everyone has its advantages. You're bold in trying new things because if you fail, no one knows. Besides, what's there to lose? A nothing can lose nothing.

Occasionally you're called upon to make an appearance for
your teachers, parents and friends. You don a bright coat that
gives you dimension along with a mask that's friendly and
appealing. As you move among them disguised to look like them,
they acknowledge your presence, smile, and make conversation.
You can act like that, too because you've watched so closely for
so long. You know the words to say and expressions to use. You
know to remain a respectful distance, rather than rush in with
empathy and passion, which might scare them. If they offer you
compliments, you politely decline. If they hurl an insult, the
negativity sails through your nothingness, no harm done. If they
express an interest in getting to know you, you gently rebuff
them. They obviously don't know how you've tricked them into
liking your manufactured shine. Any compliment they offer is
not for you, but instead for your glossy exterior. When they
express a desire to know you, they mean the exciting fake you,
not the dull real one.

You never think of taking off your costume because if you do,
they'd see nothing, and how boring.

But as you grow, where you were once a happy-go-lucky
ghost, you now feel trapped. You're inside a cramped costume
that every day grows more restrictive. You have so many ideas
in your head, yet you have no one with whom to share them.
Specifically, you have no right to burden anyone because you
have nothing to offer them, not really. That and they'll feel
cheated if you reveal how you've tricked them into thinking of
you as a sparkly gem rather than a common rock. Lastly, you
can't load them with your weighty feelings because now they're
used to your breezy repetition of *I'm fine*. You've learned people
prefer those who are happy and uncomplicated.

To your husband, you're dressed as a woman who doesn't
embarrass him or spend too much money. To your kids, you're a

vehicle. You transport their bodies, give them food, offer encouragement and fill them with knowledge about how to survive in the world. But you don't show them who you really are either because you assume they won't care.

Your casing grows tight, then tighter, until you're worried about exploding out of your hiding place. You've even stopped talking to your sisters because now you're so full of shit that if you do explode, you'll cover them with crap and add to the challenges they face.

You walk around like this, your interior stiff from immobility and the pressure of your professional exterior. Your appearance still exudes calm and well-being, which apparently succeeds because people smile at you and ask your opinion. You hear the serenity in your voice—everything fine, so fine—when the sound you want to make is a rasping squawk because you're gasping for air.

And you get in the car and you drive to your dad's house and you sit and he talks and talks as you pulse with poor circulation and wonder how all of this will end.

Then your dad looks at you.

And he doesn't look at your fancy exterior either. Instead, he pierces through that falsehood to the very center of you and confirms what no one else seems to know, but that he has always known, that you're nothing.

Why would she want to do that, just go to see you?

Rather than explode, you implode.

Because you're nothing, there's no sound. You simply become a blob of ghostly, floating gas that spreads out. Despite the silence and slow-moving, almost artistic nature of this calamity, you're distressed by this helpless, gaseous state. You start whispering to the air around you.

Hello. Anybody out there? If you can hear me, I don't feel so good.

And amazingly enough, a voice says, *You don't?*

Nope. I'm ... I don't know what happened, but ...

Can you talk about it?

No, not really. Because it's weird. I was wrapped up nicely. Now I'm blown all over the place and I have no idea how I'll come together again.

Well I'm glad you're telling me.

I'm telling you? You mean you're not a voice in my head? But I guess that's a stupid thing to say, because I don't have a head. Which means ... You're a separate entity, and you can hear me?

Yes to both.

You can hear the real me, whatever that is? This stuff that's floating around?

Yes, though you don't look like you're floating around.

But I feel like that.

Okay.

But I'm not?

No.

What do I look like?

Like a human. Head, arms, legs. The works.

And I look around and see that over the course of this strange conversation, I've somehow attained a form. The gas has collected into a distinct human shape that appears new to me. The skin feels raw because there's no coating of protection. The sun, the wind, they come at me with their fists. I look across the porch to where my sister, Dee, sits.

She looks concerned.

"I just made an appointment with a therapist," I say.

"I think that's a good idea," she says.

—

While I found only a few articles about the experience of neuro-typical children of ASD parents, that was enough to let me know there are thousands, maybe millions, of others challenged by the repercussions of their parents' seemingly invisible, undiagnosed condition.

"An Asperger's parent might say everything is fine. They're not aware of any problem for their child. However, there's that Catch 22. Neurologically, they are unable to be aware of it. But that doesn't mean there isn't a problem," wrote Jody Smith in *Asperger's Parents and Neurotypical Children* (EmpowerHer.com, 2009).

She went on to write:

> Children assume, and internalize, that there is some-thing wrong with them, that it is somehow their fault when their parents can't show them love and affection in non-verbal ways they can understand. To compound the situation, Asperger's was unheard of at that time.

> Many offspring of Aspies are dogged throughout their lives with depression and low self-worth. In their early lives their thoughts and feelings weren't acknowledged so the ability to develop healthy rela-tionships later in life was stunted.

> They don't expect to be heard. They don't expect to be understood. They have no frame of reference for it. And though they don't have the Asperger's neurolog-ical profile, some never learned how to fully express and receive love and affection for those around them, and so the ripples of isolation spread.

I've also learned there are a variety of reasons people feel as invisible as I once did. In an article titled *The Loneliness and Shame of Feeling Invisible: How to Find Your Voice* (*PsychCentral*, June 14, 2019), Dr. Margaret Rutherford suggests chronic depression can make us feel others don't care about us. Or we may live in cultures that undervalue or ignore our race, age, gender, ethnicity, or economic or marital status. Those same factors may encourage us to hide to avoid prejudice. And sometimes we may be seen only for what we do, or the condition we have, rather than as a person. Consider the nail girl, the pool guy, the heart rehab dude.

Dr. Rutherford includes four reasons kids can turn into little Caspers. The first is they grow up feeling or being told they're not the favorite child. The second, their parents have an addiction or mental illness that's so scary for kids, they instinctively hide. Thirdly, if parents are extremely busy or emotionally detached, children can become emotionally neglected. Lastly, in chaotic households, kids might give themselves the job of being *the good child* who balances the chaos with calm. In my own case, I'll never know exactly what led to my state of invisibility, but the last three reasons seem plausible.

An article titled *You Feel Invisible and Alone (and What to do About It)* (FoundationsCounselingLLC.com) states, "In order to feel loved, respected and validated, we need to feel comfortable feeling and expressing our emotions. Ideally, this emotional development will occur during childhood. Otherwise, children are more likely to feel invisible as they get older. These feelings then continue through adulthood."

The article goes on to say:

> The solution to feeling invisible isn't always easy, especially if the reasons are beyond your control.

But, that doesn't mean it's impossible to rid yourself of feelings of invisibility and inadequacy. In fact, many people feel invisible to others because they are invisible to themselves. They ignore their own feelings, put others' needs above their own and accept one-sided relationships as the norm.

Once you understand what makes you feel this way, and why the emotions are so strong, you can begin to heal.

–

You can begin to heal.
When I read those words, I thought, *That would be nice.*

The House

Once there was a house.
Once there was a choice.

The house was made of inside,
while the choice lived outside.

Before that, there were many other choices,
all outside, too, but
that could be gotten to

because the house had a
door that opened, allowing a going out
and a coming in, and had, and did.

But then came this choice, of surprise
and delight and innocence,
more than any other.

A choice made wholly of outside,
it could not come in, but rather must be
gone to and embraced.

Surprise. Delight. Innocence.
Yet a choice to which the responsible
door should not open.

The house suddenly so bounded, so
permanent, so ...
shut.

The windows, with their crosshatched bars,
gazed out at the choice,

though really, a choice
no more, but instead
a reverie,

forever out there.

One of the therapists I called in that moment of crisis at my sister's house was an older woman who told me she'd been practicing for thirty years and loved helping people. I told her my dad may have undiagnosed ASD, which possibly messed me up. She told me her stepson was on the spectrum, so she was familiar with the disorder. We made an appointment. Quietly, desperately, I waited for ten days to attend my first-ever therapy session. I envisioned walking in, sitting down and explaining the Armageddon of my interior world.

I should have known something was wrong when the therapist began the session by talking about herself. The longer she talked, the more I realized she wasn't going to help me, which made me sadder and more desperate than when I entered. Coming from a journalism background, I should have understood finding a therapist would be similar to covering a story: you have to check a variety of sources before determining which experts are reliable. But as a drowning person, I'd grasped the hand of whoever had been closest.

About twenty minutes into a session where she talked most of the time, I was close to telling her we should stop the session.

But then she said, "I think I know what's wrong."

I leaned forward out of a mix of curiosity and internal frenzy, which made me vulnerable in a way I'd never been before.

The woman waited for a dramatic pause, then smiled and said, "You're on the spectrum."

My heart sprinted. Drums beat in my head. I didn't blink or move as she reiterated the words I'd used to describe my situation, complaining they lacked emotion.

I heard myself answer, "I'm not sure what you're talking about. I said I was *sad* and *angry* and *hurting*. How, exactly, do those words lack emotion? What other words could I have used?"

Now she looked a little nervous, but said, "You seem a little remote."

Had I been on an even keel, I would have told her what I now know. *I can see why you'd think that. My guess is I've learned the communication habits of a parent who may have had ASD, and so appear to have the neurological disorder.*

But I wasn't calm. I wasn't level-headed. I wasn't thinking clearly. I'd been wrestling and struggling and stressing for so long to handle the side effects of my dad's apparent disability that her comment felt like the final, gentle shove that could push me over the edge. But I refused to submit. I tightened everything inside and for a moment, stopped moving and breathing.

Balanced in perfect equilibrium, one foot on the cliff, one foot off, I said in a voice as calm as possible, "You lack the credentials to diagnose someone."

The woman paused. As she stared at me, I could see in her eyes the doubt, that maybe she'd overstepped her bounds. She began to equivocate.

I interrupted, "My sister is a speech pathologist. She works with kids on the spectrum. A diagnosis doesn't come about until a whole team of people test the kid. Thoroughly. Hours, days, lots of evaluations. You don't have the training to make such a pronouncement."

Now she understood the implication of my words, that her license might be at risk.

The heat of my interior melted my icy exterior and flames launched from my mouth.

"I came here to tell you how my self-worth got pummeled by a dad with possible autism and you have the audacity to then—with no expertise—tell me I have the same condition, when someone who really has ASD probably wouldn't have noticed any of this shit? I mean, my god, I come in here for help and you strike me with the very weapon that's been used against me? If a woman comes in complaining her husband beats her, what do you do, tell her she deserves it?"

I stood up. I pulled money from my wallet for the co-pay as she babbled apologies and that I shouldn't worry about paying. But I heard my under-water-sounding voice tell her I never wanted to be in debt to someone like her.

Since my dad had taught me not to cry, what came out were great heaves, as though I'd been sprinting and someone shoved me sideways, causing me to stagger and lurch and lose the rhythm of my breathing.

I had to drive home along back streets because I was so upset my vision blurred, making me think of my Grandma Edith who'd gone blind for a time during her breakdown. I drove twenty-five miles an hour with both hands on the wheel while shifting my eyes right and left. Yet everywhere I looked, that stupid woman was in front of me. Someone who'd been practicing for thirty years. Someone who claimed to love helping people. How many people had she destroyed through incompetence of which she seemed oblivious?

Fortunately, though I was vulnerable, I wasn't stupid. I had enough information to stop her absurd claims. But what about someone who didn't have that knowledge? Someone who, instead of a childhood filled with the love and kindness my parents had shown me, had been treated terribly and might be vulnerable to swallowing the therapist's utter shit?

I pulled into my driveway. I got out and called Dee and told her about the session. About how as a kid I never opened myself to people for the obvious reason that would give them ammunition to hurt me, and here I finally found the courage to override that belief, only to be proven right. To have my own story used against me. To be violated and made to feel even less than nothing. I walked back and forth in the late afternoon sun while talking and talking. She said I could lodge a complaint with the state licensing board and I nodded, knowing I should.

But this was the closest I'd come to a full mental breakdown. Panting, I paced, drinking in air, yet drowning. Where only months before at my mother's funeral I had a rock-solid life, I was now—

Fucking broken.

And the question came: how could my mother know me if I didn't know me? The dutiful daughter, wife, mother, all of that had been a lie because I'd been raised to lie. *It's fine, it's fine, it's so goddamned fine!* So that now I didn't know how not to lie to myself.

When in this kind of real-life emotional inferno, the world roars, your body jackhammers, and everything around you crumbles. I literally hung onto reality by the hand that gripped the phone, my lifeline to one of the few people in the world who listened and understood.

I didn't lodge any complaint against that therapist.

–

I found a second therapist. This time I sent her a list of the coping and communication skills I wanted to learn and asked if she could help. She said yes. Over the course of the four sessions we managed to fit in before her retirement, I laid out the symptoms of dishonesty, loneliness and isolation and asked for specific ways to rid myself of the chronic pain and bad habits I'd learned. She was kind, helpful and didn't overstep the boundaries I set.

I could have been more open with her. After she retired, I should have continued therapy, a concept that had been taboo in my youth but I now thought of as personal training for the heart and mind. At least she got me started in the right direction.

But I was by no means in the clear yet.

Part V
Marriage and Children

People say

Be honest,
but you think, *there's no fucking way.*

So when they say, *Bring your*
child, so we can see.

You say, *No, that's okay.*

They say, *No really.*

You say, *Yeah, really.*

They say, *We want*
to meet the kid.

You say, *No, you don't.*

You just
don't know better.
You don't know why you don't
want to meet my kid. You don't know
how you don't want to meet what grew

inside me. What I bring forth only when I'm alone,
only for myself. Some people can't look, can't see, can't
appreciate the terrible beauty, but I glory in knowing who I am,
who I made, the strength, the destructive ability, the guilelessness of

a being just...

being

a thing just a thing

what you feel a fact

that when you're alone, toddles out

arms raised to you, smiling, no idea

of its hideousness, and you promise no

one will have this child, no one

will destroy what is part of you, what

they'd rear back from, horrified, hurt, devastated,

until demanding you kill

the monster, and you say, *But you wanted—*

*No we didn't. Not that. It isn't true. We don't want
to know.*

And you say, *Okay,*
and tuck the child back,
away.

But that's only if you did
what they asked.

Which you don't.

When the time came to leave for my freshman year of college, Sue and I loaded our belongings into our old station wagon, which our family had nicknamed *The Blue Bomb*, a vehicle with an appearance that matched its name. We took off in the morning before first light and drove from New Jersey straight through to my university in Missouri. She helped me tote boxes to my dorm room, hugged and kissed me and took off for her college in Illinois, a few hours' drive back along the interstate we'd just taken.

Then college life began. I met my roommate and the girls on my floor and we walked everywhere to check out everything. We gathered in groups to go for meals in the cafeteria. To keep costs down, I only called my parents every two weeks and talked to my sisters about as often.

Dorm meetings, classes, working in the cafeteria, interviewing people for the student newspaper, going to parties. Though nerve-wracking and exhausting to be thrown into so many new circumstances, I had a great time. But I also began to feel what I hadn't before, a strange emptiness. Why would I feel lonely around so many people?

I didn't know then what I do now, that my existence to this point in my life had depended on remaining closely connected to my sisters. But in college, I had no deep connections and my previous survival techniques began to falter. And because I didn't feel comfortable letting anyone see the real me, and because I'd become used to pretending nothing was wrong, I prevented any chance of developing significant friendships.

My loneliness grew to a crushing emptiness akin to a deep and persistent chest cold, though without the cough. I wished I could put a fist on my sternum and apply enough pressure to make the almost physical burning go away. But at every turn, I was reminded that though among people I knew and laughed with and saw every day, I was not part of their lives in any significant way. I was on the outside, where I'd always been most comfortable, but that now felt terrible. Maybe other students felt the same for any number of reasons. I never found out, though, because I didn't share my feelings, which would have invited them to share theirs. All I understood was I didn't have a right to burden others. And because my complaints didn't rate compared to the terrible traumas some people suffered, I didn't consider therapy. Counselors should spend their time helping people who struggled with serious issues like depression and suicidal thoughts rather than some small, petty problem I couldn't describe. The best contribution I could make in a turbulent world was to be self-sufficient, as in a person who offered help rather than asked for it. I'd always solved my problems before and would do so again without anyone's assistance.

But this time I couldn't. Though I socialized a lot, I couldn't connect with people and didn't know why. I rechecked my expressions, gestures and conduct, but all were socially acceptable. Something else—something invisible—set me apart from them. Something I didn't want to live with. Something that was wrong.

Then I met Mike.

In my sophomore year, I had no money to travel to New Jersey for spring break. Even if I could have afforded one of the expensive spring break trips to South Padre Island in Texas, I had no interest in the beer-chugging, wet T-shirt-wearing chaos. In a pinch, I could find a ride to St. Louis two hours away and stay with Grandma Margaret in Alton, where I could also visit with my aunt and cousins. But I longed for a more exciting experience. While looking through the student newspaper, I read a cartoony advertisement about a backpacking trip to the Ozarks, the hilly southwestern part of Missouri. I'd never backpacked before or been to that part of the state. And at sixty dollars, the trip was the cheapest option I had. I wrote my check and signed up at the Student Outdoor Adventure Club Office.

But then I got worried I'd be one female in the boonies among a dozen huge, testosterone-charged males. So I called the trip leader, Mike.

I immediately didn't like his higher-pitched voice. And when I asked if I'd be the only female, he laughed at me. He clearly didn't have sisters or otherwise understand that women have to be constantly vigilant about their safety. When he stopped laughing, he explained he'd been running these trips for the last few years and the groups primarily consisted of women. As a journalist in training, I remained skeptical.

At the orientation meeting, an energized, smiling Mike handed out an equipment list and told us we'd travel in a club-owned van. As he talked about other logistics, I evaluated my trekking mates: seven females and one guy. I gave Mike a point.

I bought the cheapest pair of hiking boots I could find, purchased a pair of wool pants and gloves from a military surplus store in town, and gathered the remaining items. A few days before the trip, the other eight participants and I hiked our gear to the basement of Mike's fraternity. He moved amongst us to check our equipment and make suggestions about what to leave or add. He explained the van had broken down. Fortunately, two people in our group had offered to drive their vehicles. One car would be left at our trailhead, and the other at our destination. At the end of our trip, two people would drive to retrieve the car from the trailhead, then return, pick us up and we'd continue home.

I watched and listened carefully for clues about what kind of leader Mike would be. Coming from an all-female family, I automatically evaluated men to determine if they could be trusted, especially those who'd be in charge of my safety.

Fortunately, Mike didn't seem to belong to what I considered the most dangerous type of guy Mom called *a charmer,* or a guy who emotionally manipulates others to get what he wants. Nor did Mike *run hot and cold,* pleasant one minute and irritable the next, which would decrease the need to tread lightly. Instead, Mike appeared to be a straightforward guy, as in *what you see is what you get.* In particular, my organized heart appreciated his precision and sense of responsibility.

On departure day, we packed and took off on what would—and still is—the worst trip of my life.

Amy, the young woman who volunteered to drive Mike and me, drove like she talked: in a fast, swerving manner. If we'd traveled during the day on a straight road, the experience would have been only mildly hair-raising. But we were on a twisty, unlit, two-lane mountain road on a black night during a raging thunderstorm. I sat in the back. To keep myself from being thrown side to side, I lodged one hand on the side door and the other on the roof. Intensely anxious, I distracted myself by making small talk.

In the calmest tone I could muster, I asked Mike that most typical of college questions, "What's your major?"

And again he laughed. A real hyena, this guy.

"Physics," he said.

"Physics?"

Laughing, he said, "What, did you think I was a forestry major or something?"

Which was exactly what I'd thought. Who wouldn't make that assumption, judging by how much he obviously loved backpacking? He went on to tell me he'd graduate in a month and attend graduate school in the fall. And so we talked and swerved and gasped and talked as the rain poured.

Our group stopped at a bar to use the bathroom. We made a wide circle around two women fighting in the muddy parking lot. When we reconvened outside beneath an overhang, a drunk dude tried to pick a fight with a woman in our group. Driving on, we didn't arrive until three a.m. We got soaked pitching our tents. As we slept, Mike and the two drivers, Carolyn and Amy, drove to where our hike would end. They left Carolyn's car and returned in Amy's. Now about six a.m., Mike roused us to pack and start hiking. Amy proved to be the slowest hiker in our group, which made staying warm in the fifty-degree Fahrenheit weather almost impossible. The rain didn't stop. My mittens dripped water, steady as a faucet. Creeks swelled into raging torrents.

After the third long day of hiking in the rain, I sat in my tiny tent with my tentmate. I struggled to get out of my sodden clothes to less-sodden clothes. My fingertips remained white from the cold and pruney from the constant dampness. I was sick of all the shitty beauty outside—the trees, the rocks, the various critters no doubt running around happily—and wished I'd gone to Alton. Staying with my grandma in her senior apartment building would have been high living. I determined not to leave the tent again for the night, meaning this would be the night I learned to pee in a bottle.

Then a voice outside said, "Hey."

I looked through the mesh door to see Mike's vague shape. I unzipped the screen and looked into his smiling face. Bending over, he extended a hand holding an open Cup O' Noodles, steam rising from the hot water he'd added to bring those crappy dried soup ingredients to life. "Dinner."

I've since been lucky enough to eat many fancy meals and have enjoyed every one. But I have never so appreciated a culinary moment as when Mike handed me that cheap Styrofoam cup of hot, salty goodness. Looking into his smiling eyes, I wanted to take his face in my hands and plant a kiss on his cheek, my heart filled with gratitude to someone who'd stayed outside in the cold and wet and growing dark to make sure I, and the rest of us, got fed something hot. He was clearly a young man who didn't drop the ball; he was a leader who'd take care of us and who could be trusted.

The next morning before breakfast, I followed the trail down to a creek we were supposed to cross. The waterway had become a fifteen-foot-wide firehose of whitewater. Other people came down until we were all gathered to stare at this final outrage perpetrated by nature against our group. None of us spoke for a long moment.

I looked at Mike, who was smiling a little, and said, "I'm not crossing that."

He laughed and said, "Well, fortunately there's no reason to."

Carolyn, the young woman beside him, grinned with embarrassment and said, "I left my keys in Amy's car."

Blinking rain from my eyelashes, I stammered, "So, so—" I swallowed and tried again, "So what you're saying is that all this time, we've been hiking toward a car we can't get into?"

I don't know who started laughing first, but within a few beats, everybody's mouth had blown open to emit that desperate sound known as hysterical laughter. We packed up and over the next two days slogged back to our starting point.

And through all of that, Mike never stopped smiling. He never stopped offering encouragement. He never stopped finding solutions for broken laces or other faulty gear. His cheerfulness didn't stem from a polite need to cover uncomfortable moments or convey an image of *I'm fine*, but instead from enjoyment of an adventure that literally and proverbially included both rain and sun. We arrived back on campus three days before spring break ended. I arranged to spend the remainder of that time with my grandma. Mike and his friend, both of whom lived in St. Louis, gave me a ride to the city's airport, where my cousin would pick me up.

At the airport, Mike got out to help schlepp my gear to the curb. He smiled at me. I took his face in my hands and planted a kiss on his cheek.

—

At some point after we started dating, Mike and I were arguing about something I no longer wanted to talk about. I changed the subject, the strategy my mom used to redirect my dad when he got agitated.

Mike stared at me. "Did you just change the subject like I wouldn't notice?"

I stared at him, shocked and outraged. Yes, I did change the subject to distract him. And yes, I did not expect him to notice.

My dad never noticed, but instead would charge on in the new direction, at which point Mom would wink at me.

What was the matter with Mike? Why didn't he act normal?

Before Mike, whenever I got upset, I'd disappear with my diary, write fervently about the injustice perpetrated against me, and freeze out the offender for as long as necessary for the person to get the message. Holding a grudge never worked with my dad, however, because he never noticed I was upset. Even if he noticed my sullen demeanor, he probably wouldn't have considered he'd been the source of my angst. But the approach worked for everyone else.

Except for Mike. Rather than leave me alone, he'd doggedly follow, asking *What's the matter, what's wrong, how come you can't say, just try to say, just spit it out.* Worse, he'd physically hold me, I'd wriggle out of his grasp, and he'd grab me again, until exhausted, I'd spit out the problem. Then he'd say, *Okay,* as in, *problem noted.* If the problem called for a practical solution, he'd find one. Incident over, he'd soon be smiling again.

And I had to admit, though only to myself, that spitting out an ugly issue took a lot less energy than holding onto the unhappiness.

We got married. We bought a house and had two kids. Life got busy and stressful.

I don't know what else to say, other than that the compaction of time, physical living space and the emotional needs of the many provide a warm, dark, moist haven for emotional infections to take hold and flourish in those inclined to keep everything inside, like me.

With two kids and a mortgage and the need to grind along, Mike had less energy and time to encourage me to voice a problem. And therein began the accumulation of anger and resentment that affects many couples and which thickens like a choking mucus.

Sometimes I had an elusive issue I needed to discuss and thereby clarify. But when Mike came home from his job as a software engineer, he did so after a day of helping others figure out their problems. He only had a few hours in which to take care of bills or other business. He needed quiet time but had little kids running around, drawing on his attention. Both of us were tired and irritable and would muddle through until the kids went to bed, often forgetting or putting off important discussions, sometimes indefinitely. Faced with only enough time to take care of business, we neglected letting one another know what we felt inside.

As in:

He comes in the back door from work. I'm sitting at the table and tell him we need to set aside time to talk.

"About what?" he says, unpacking the backpack he wears when biking to work.

"Just ... stuff. We never talk about anything that matters."

"I just got home! What do you want to talk about?"

"What, like you want me to give you headlines?"

"That would be good."

"Forget it."

"No. Talk."

"No, let's just do like normal and talk business. The window guy came to give an estimate."

"How much does he want?"

And so it went.

—

I always thought if I ever gave up writing, watch out. I had no illusions the act of silently spewing into my journal or writing stories on a regular basis kept me even-keeled. By then, I'd had a play produced in Hollywood, a dozen short stories published in literary magazines and a first novel published. But enough time had passed, I began to feel anxious for another success to validate both the time I spent writing and my worth as a person. After rewriting my second novel, *Winter Light*, I began submitting to literary agents with high hopes. My fifteen-year-old character of Mary Donahue deserved to have her story told.

Five agents.

Ten.

Twenty.

Seventy-eight.

A hundred-and-seventy-eight.

I stopped submitting. I stopped writing.

Mike and I were coming up on our twenty-fifth wedding anniversary. We had a son in high school and a daughter in college. I remember thinking, *This is cool. This is all right. I'm feeling pretty good. And how awesome our years together have passed quickly and more or less happily and how fine, fine, fine.*

All spoken in that scary-clown inner voice.

Though diagnosed with terminal cancer, Mom smiled too, insisting she was fine, fine, fine.

I started bike riding in a big way with a client, now friend. Two hours, three hours, five hours, so that by the end of those adventures, sheer exhaustion released at least some of my built-up anxiety and unnamed anger. Mike and I spoke less often, he due to work stress and me from not wanting to invite criticism for tasks I didn't perform with the same precision he'd apply: putting back a tool I'd used, recording a check I'd written, storing something in the right place in the garage. Errors that would inflame the bad habits he'd inherited from his Eastern European ancestry, of never offering compliments for what you do well, but instead believing other people purposely make mistakes to ruin your day.

I traveled east to be with Mom and Dad during that last big radiation treatment in New York City. I went again in the fall when she almost died from dehydration. And I went again in November as my dad insisted to Mom, *Swallow, Norm, just swallow.*

Then she died. And never knew me. Because I'd lied to her. Because I felt she wanted me to lie and had taught me how to do it. *Fine, fine!* Then Mike wanted to retire at a young age, saying he'd watched our pennies carefully, and according to his calculation, had saved enough to never work again. Yet before that moment, I had no idea he wanted to retire, let alone he'd been steering toward that financial path. I was horrified by the prospect of being on a budget with a person who didn't like to do anything I did: travel, bike, hike, or even occasionally eat at fancy restaurants.

And then I went to visit Dad.

Why would she want to just see you?

A few months later, I passed Mike on my way out of the house. He asked where I was going and I said, "You can hide whatever you want from people and they'll never know."

"What do you mean?" he said from where he sat on the couch. "What are you hiding?"

"Everything."

"I don't know what that means."

"We're no longer a team."

"Yes we are."

"Nope. You've been so critical for so long that I don't want to tell you anything anymore. Nothing meaningful, anyway. I don't know how to say anything."

"What does that *mean?*"

"Let me think about it."

And I left for whatever outing I'd devised to distract me for at least another few hours.

I'd stopped trying to communicate with Mike about my internal world. If I didn't tell him how I felt, how could he know?

So I started talking.

And it was really shitty.

And Mike held on.

—

When Mom taught me how to change a subject smoothly, without the other person noticing, the skill became my main survival strategy. If people focused too much attention on me, I told them something I truly admired about them and they redirected to the story behind that attribute or success. Relieved, I'd sit back and enjoy listening.

But Mike didn't allow me to hide or run away. Our friendship began when he put his spotlight on me and kept it there. Though true, the child-rearing years derailed us from paying close attention to one another, presumably a typical story for most couples, when I finally rang the warning bell, he refocused on me.

I had to change too. Until my discovery about the psychological impact of Dad's possible ASD, I often played the martyr who didn't have the right to make a fuss. Now I not only had the right to speak up, but the duty because if you don't bring up important issues, you might miss the opportunity to help others connect, share their experiences and, ultimately, heal.

A case in point is Jody Smith's 2009 article, which spurred so many responses over the coming years that in 2015 she wrote a follow-up article describing the feedback she'd received (*NT Children of Parents With Aspergers: Looking for Information?*, EmpowerHer.com, 2015). Some of the responses came from ASD parents who objected to the idea their neurological difference might harm the self-esteem of their NT children, an understandable reaction given how besieged autistic people are by criticism from the world around them. But the overwhelming majority of responses came from NT kids who'd since grown up.

Smith writes:

> The cry that I heard over and over again was, thank you for remembering us. Thank you for telling me I'm not alone.

> Thank you for telling me I am not the cause of this depression, loneliness, sorrow, grief. Thank you for helping me to understand where all that pain has come from.

> Thank you for suggesting I can hope for something better, because it wasn't me after all. Thank you for saying it's OK for me to open my mouth and speak, and expect to be heard, to be visible to other people.

> It's OK to expect, to require, something for myself in my relationships. It's OK for me to hold out for being an equal participant, and equally on the receiving end. Thanks for the reassurance that wanting such things is not selfish, it's just human, and part of any healthy relationship.

In relearning to communicate with Mike, I dropped all attempts to play the cheerful hostess. To *look at the bright side* or *beat around the bush* or *find the right moment*. I thought about what needed to be said, put myself in front of Mike, and forced myself to say those things clearly and without anger or using mean words. My message came down to this: though I knew he loved me, he often said and did things that made me feel insignificant; words, habits and actions I'd no longer stand for.

He not only listened but *heard* I was changing, which meant he had to change too, before it was too late. When I made an error, he no longer treated me like someone out to ruin his day. He no longer *teased* me, that age-old method of disguising hurtful opinions as humor. He listened more. He began apologizing when he should. He helped more.

Things improved some.

I rode my bike, went to yoga, learned to surf and began writing and writing. I wasn't home much. When I got home, he was there.

He retired. His stress disappeared. He relaxed and got happier and more helpful by taking over the grocery shopping and doing the majority of cooking. He fixed my computer. He glued a magnet doorstop to my office door to keep it from closing. When I got a flat on my bike, he fixed the tire. If I needed something at the store, he'd stop to get it. He became cheerful backpacker Mike instead of stressed programmer Mike.

At night in bed, he listened in silence to what I felt. Sad, hurt, angry, sometimes at him, sometimes at my parents, disappointed with myself, overwhelmed by all I'd been holding inside.

We started to be a team again, an outcome I don't believe we would have reached had he not retired and found the time and energy to reconnect to his compassion and joy in life.

And to me.

On our anniversary a year after Mom died, Mike and I went away for the weekend. On a warm, sunny May evening, we walked to a restaurant where sliding doors opened onto a garden. Sitting on a couch in the bar area, we ordered burgers.

I told Mike about a client who volunteered for a nonprofit organization that helps at-risk teens improve their future. The previous year she'd been assigned a teen girl and worked with her on better study habits and problem-solving skills, while also taking her on fun outings to lighten the load of obstacles she faced. But despite a variety of efforts involving several social agencies, the girl kept returning to her father for guidance, even though he was the biggest impediment to her advancement. He didn't encourage her to do homework or get a job and had an unsupportive, critical attitude. My client wondered why the girl would choose to remain tethered to such a negative source over the chance for a brighter future.

When she voiced the question, an answer popped into my head. At some level, maybe the girl understood help from strangers was fleeting. At least with her dad, she could count on him to keep her clothed, fed and housed, the basics of survival. In exchange, she put up with his negative behavior, and maybe even felt she deserved the criticism.

"So I was thinking about that," I told Mike, "and realized that must be how abuse victims feel. The reason they go back to their abusers is because while social workers and other well-intentioned people might say things like, *You're such a good person and you have so much potential*, the victims just nod, knowing those people are trying to help, but clearly don't know any better. The do-gooders can't see the truth, what the victims know: they really are nothing. And that's what binds them to their abusers.

Though life is shitty and chaotic, there's one thing they can rely on, their abusers knowing the truth about them."

"How would you know that?" Mike said.

"Because that's what it's been like. With my dad and how it messed things up in my head. I look at people. I hear them smiling and saying good things about me and offering compliments, but I can't believe the things they say because I know the truth. I'm not much of anything."

"Well that's fucked up."

I nodded.

—

While visiting the East Coast a few months later, my sister, Dee, and I went kayaking on a Connecticut lake. Afterward, we stopped at a hilltop winery. A renovated barn at the intersection of two country lanes, the surrounding grounds had been beautifully landscaped with wildflowers and a rock garden. While roaming around, I walked up the drive to where we entered. Oak trees heavily shaded the bumpy, unlined road we'd arrived on. On the other side of that darkness, a light-filled vision of splendor flowed outward: a golden sun bathing a lush green valley cooled by a blue lake. Paradise, but over there, just out of reach.

I glance up at the street sign. *Bliss Road.*

I took a photo, not of the ethereal landscape, but of the worn and scratched metal signpost. Walking back to the winery, I thought about what Sue had said so long ago about writing a book containing what she hadn't known about autism but now did.

When I reached Dee, I said, "I'm going to write a memoir about all of this and name it *Bliss Road.*"

"Good name," she said.

I didn't start writing the book that day, or even in the following months. If I had, I wouldn't have been able to finish the story because I still didn't know then what I do now.

I hadn't fully crossed that narrow, treacherous road. Not yet.

Eight more years passed in which I went down, down, down. Then I fought my way back up, grasping at every outstretched hand friends and family offered. After the nauseating tumble of that psychological fun house, I stumbled around for a while before the dizziness wore off and I could right myself enough to carry on. I thought my life would stabilize. But one more head-snapping spin had yet to occur.

After understanding how my self-esteem had been damaged, I began to realize the extent to which I'd harmed those of my kids.

Part VI
Reckoning

a poem in 60 heartbeats

Reckoning

you know when you're
looking at a little kid?
at the top of his head,
because he's looking down
at a bug in his hand and
you think, oh no,
and you say calm things
like, *be careful now, you*
don't want to—
then squish,
and he looks up
like he doesn't know
what happened because
he doesn't,
and nobody tells you
that could be you some
day, a loving parent
loving so hard you
squish
those guileless eyes
staring up at you

The issues my dad's possible ASD caused me could largely be attributed to poor timing.

To start with, autism didn't become a widely known disability until he'd become a grandfather.

If my dad had been diagnosed early in life, he and those around him would have had a name for what made him think and behave differently than others. Due to assessments and help from experts, he would have understood what he excelled at and the skills he needed to learn. He could have explained the neurological condition so people like my mom could better interpret his actions and use different tactics to communicate with him.

Ideally, Mom and Dad would have taken specialized parenting classes. Instructors could have coached Dad on how to bond with my sisters and me from birth by adopting daily parent-child sessions that involve smiling, talking, playing with and cuddling kids, all of which helps babies feel safe and assured of consistent kindness. Instructors could have shown Mom how to neutralize conflicts and help Dad more accurately interpret our actions. She could have explained Dad's ASD so we understood why he sometimes acted as he did, and more importantly, learn what triggered him and the actions to soothe him, all of which would have helped us protect ourselves.

Those two actions—getting assessed for ASD and taking part in specialized parenting classes—could help families flourish. To my knowledge, no such parenting classes exist, though I hope this book encourages mental health providers and educators to see how such relatively simple steps could reduce the number of people requiring therapy later in life. Such guidance seems particularly prudent at this point in time, given those who were first diagnosed as children following the creation of the diagnosis in 1994 have now reached the average age of parenthood.

If Dad had been assessed and been prepared for parenthood, I have no doubt I would have developed a healthy psychological and emotional foundation. My sisters and I would have been able to attribute his behavior to ASD, rather than internalize his hurtful words and actions, and we would have known to speak up. As a family, we could have developed healthier communication strategies and so reduce emotional trauma. When my sisters and I got married, maybe we would have thought more deeply about having kids. While I love every person in my family and believe the world is a better place for the talent and perspective they offer, I also believe couples have a duty to contemplate the likelihood of known genetic possibilities, and if they decide to have children, have a plan for addressing those challenges.

Yet *maybe* and *what if* scenarios are not reality.

My nephew, Brian, for example, was among the first children to receive an Asperger's diagnosis. Yet many educators didn't know much about ASD. As a result of their negativity toward him, as well as that of other kids, he expressed thoughts of suicide as early as age six. My sister went the extra mile by typing up a fact sheet about ASD, the specific behaviors Brian exhibited, and strategies for successfully communicating with him. She gave the document to his teachers but doubted they read the information, judging by the irritation with which they talked about Brian during parent-teacher meetings. The school district did follow standardized rules that gave him extra time on tests and allowed him to do homework in a quiet room to cut down on distractions that aggravated his ADHD. But he didn't receive the instruction he needed most, social interaction coaching. That instruction could have helped him identify what was happening in any given situation while offering actual verbal scripts to follow. For example, if someone asks, *Can I get you anything?*, learning to change a response from a perfunctory *No*, to *No, thank you*, can help people be perceived as gracious, rather than rude, because the *thank you* acknowledges the kindness of the initial offer.

High school intensified Brian's growing sense of anger and isolation. The number of students and more chaotic classrooms exacerbated his ADHD. He was surrounded by adolescents whose advancing neurological development helped them more clearly see differences in those around them, and in turn exploit any oddness as a means of boosting their as-yet shaky self-esteems. Worse still, when my sister requested meetings with the teachers, guidance counselors and principal, she learned none of them consulted one another about how to help Brian. He went to the nurse every day complaining of stomachaches as a way to escape the stress of his situation, yet the school nurse never thought to alert anyone. Then he began talking violently, both about others and himself.

If I was making a movie, this is the point where I'd insert a montage of my sister and her husband growing desperate after years of increasing anxiety: sleepless hours, hand-wringing, consulting with others. When my sister learned of the district's noncompliance in giving Brian the services spelled out in his Individualized Education Plan, she told the administrators they could either pay for a special boarding school for Brian, or she'd sue them.

They paid for admission to Franklin Academy, a boarding school an hour from Brian's home in Connecticut. The environment and curriculum had been designed for kids with neurological communication-related issues. Upon entry, he was told the academy's code of conduct: to respect each other, be honest, resolve conflicts non-violently, take care of each other and take care of the world.

The staff taught him the words necessary to describe what he felt, so rather than claim he had a stomachache, he learned to tell people he felt anxious, after which he learned to tell them why. And rather than be excused from responsibility, he was given the time to calm down but told when he felt better, he had to follow through with his duties. Every responsibility he exercised earned him a new freedom. Best of all, he was surrounded by people who understood, and experienced, what he had: isolation, social awkwardness, bullying, communication confusion. For the first time, he made friends.

Brian turned from an angry, isolated boy into an open, humorous, self-sufficient young man who could participate in social gatherings with nothing more than the occasional social gaff we all make. I love this kid—this man—because he, like my dad, is so good-hearted.

Brian has since graduated with a degree in engineering. He still has challenges, but he has the tools to deal with them. If others question his actions, he can explain his situation and suggest changes that'll help him participate to a greater degree.

—

Since Brian's childhood, hundreds of books, research papers and programs have shed light on autism and the unique cognitive advantages that favor methodical, logical problem-solving. In his book, *Unmasking Autism,* Dr. Price writes:

We tend not to get habituated to familiar situations or stimuli as readily as other people, so we often think through a situation as if it's completely new to us, even if it isn't. All of this requires a lot of energy, focus, and time, so we get exhausted and overloaded quite easily. However, it also makes us less prone to errors. Experimental research shows that Autistic people are far less susceptible to the biases allistic people commonly fall prey to.

While my nephew walked a tough road, he was born at a time that gave him a clear, if imperfect, path to follow: diagnosis, skills training, a productive life.

Discovery.

Help.

Better outcome.

My dad and I didn't have that mapped route.

Dad unwittingly bumped along his known road until dying in his eighties without discovering the invisible challenge that hampered his good intentions. I drove onward until almost driving off a cliff.

Finally fully awake to the once-unseen, now ludicrously obvious obstacle that stopped my forward progress, I got out of my car. I looked around. I began wandering through the wreckage leading to this point, and at the age of fifty-two, found my kids among the debris.

Fortunately, they were alive. I helped them up and wrapped my arms around them, shocked, grateful, upset, apologetic, confused and overwhelmed by my love for them.

But when I looked in their eyes, they stared back calmly but from a distance. My disorientation deepened. I thought we were all together in a wreck that happened only moments ago. But their eyes told me the truth. There was no crash. Before the disruption that shook me awake, I'd been driving what I thought was a smooth road, gazing out across a gorgeous vista, when really I'd been driving toward an abyss, my kids in tow.

the hell they'll raise

I love the hooey my kids pull, the
crackers they crumble
on my toes and
the shiny of their wet noses
gifted me with each
embrace, the shimmy of their intoxicated
hearts and silk of their tears, the
flare of their grease fires
that sear me,
leaving me

ashes

       that

             drift

on the breath of their afternoon sleep

only to stir again and swirl
in the wake of their run
past me so
fast.

I breathe them
in, where they ride
the flow of me, so interior
I feel their change
moment by millisecond,
the shout of today
different than the scratch of yesterday or
the brine of tomorrow.

My soul overtaken
by their cries of
noodle-face and
pooh-pooh head, in their
declarations of the hell
they'll raise, not knowing
they really will,
someday,

Oh, haunt my heart
always with the heart
they return so
splendidly
for the candy of my love.

I am sticky with them, and they with
Me. Touch me, my
sweets.

My husband and I moved to California when our daughter was almost two years old. One night I settled Ari into her crib and went to our bedroom to read. Minutes later I saw movement out the corner of my eye and looked up to see my daughter standing in the doorway. Pink footie pajamas, a massive head of blonde, curly hair, holding a stuffed animal tucked under her arm; she didn't say anything, but instead stared at me with the mischievous look of, *Now what are you going to do?*

And I thought, *Uh-oh.* She'd just learned how to gain her freedom, and there's no putting that genie back in the bottle.

Wearing a calm expression, I returned her to her crib. She came back to my door four more times. The exercise of climbing out must have been rigorous enough she eventually got tired and went to sleep.

The story explains everything about our daughter, whom we named Ariela, meaning *lioness of God.* And she was, and is, a lioness, complete with the flood of unruly hair and a spirit that can either make your heart swell or back you into a corner. Born to act first and think second, which later made her a great water polo player, she demanded and questioned and spoke forthright about what she felt. She exhibited an emotional courage that filled me with admiration, even when she frustrated both of us by pushing so hard against boundaries. To get attention. To get answers. To confront bullies. She didn't want to play nicely alone with dolls. She dressed in bold colors and crazy combinations and chose to be Darth Vader for Halloween. She didn't back down when challenged by teachers, problematic friends or overbearing coaches. Over time, she learned to control her passion in a way that now allows her to lead and inspire others.

My son, Colter, is almost the exact opposite. A gentle, quiet soul, his lovely eyes become upside-down moons when he smiles, just as my mom's had. Even as a little kid, he dove into solitude when contemplating something important and resurfaced far down the road with questions or conclusions that startled me. For example, when he was three years old and I sat on the edge of his bed to say goodnight, he took the opportunity to ask, "What if there is no god?" I don't recall how I responded but got the impression he found my answer lacking.

When he was five, he wandered into the kitchen to proclaim, "I don't think I'll shave." This time I felt better able to help. With his permission, I got a popsicle stick, spread some shaving cream on his soft cheeks, and let him use the edge of the stick to scrape off the lather. He agreed the experience had been manageable.

He hopped down the hall like a pogo stick. He hummed and danced in his chair when eating something he enjoyed. He had a gift for tuning in to people's emotional states. When I read Lois Lowry's *The Giver* to him over the course of a few weeks, he sat against me and listened closely, his occasional questions making clear he understood the boy's terrible predicament, that he no longer trusted his parents or believed in the ideals of his community.

My son. My daughter. They're two of the most special people in my life for the same reason most parents feel the same: kids represent the best of us. Clean, fresh, they're unmarred by the scars we grownups incur along the road to adulthood. Like most parents, I wanted nothing more than to protect my kids. I certainly didn't want to harm them.

But that's what parents do, despite their best intentions.

That unfairness is built into nature. From the moment we're born, we, like other animals are subjected to immediate threats like predators, ill weather and common accidents. And we're at the mercy of our parents. Yet when we become parents, even if we're loving, we sometimes can't see how we've injured our kids the way we were harmed.

While I might have known that in a general sense, when I became a parent, I somehow felt impervious to that outcome. After learning the damage I incurred from my parents, however, I woke to the harm I'd caused my kids.

Of the two, the latter proved a million-fold more painful. As a kid, I'd built heavy emotional armor to shield myself from pain. But as a parent, I had no safeguard against the agony of having wounded the people I love most. To the point I wondered if I'd ever get free of the guilt and shame of my blindness. To the point I wondered if there'd ever be a moment in which I found the bottom of my self-loathing.

—

There's the well-known joke about a man who's drowning and help comes his way not once, but three times via people in a rowboat, a motorboat and a helicopter, respectively. He refuses all, saying God will save him. The dude drowns. When he gets to heaven, he asks God, *Why didn't you help?* God says, *I sent you all those people! What more did you want?*

We humans exhibit the same blindness regarding our bodies. While out hiking with friends, our parched throats beg us to drink more. The discomfort in our muscles rate the terrain as too strenuous and encourages us to turn back. When we stumble on rocks, the jarring motion warns us to pick up our feet. Yet we ignore those signs. We faint. Our muscles pull. We twist our ankles.

Then we wonder why our bodies fail us.

I believe we do the same regarding our personal relationships, especially those within families. We're given so many signs: snippy comments, arguments that dampen happy moments, drama over small things. Yet we ignore or somehow miss those clues and wonder why our families are dysfunctional.

After realizing my misshapen psychological state may have harmed my kids, I looked back in time to see not just a few signs of dysfunction, but dozens.

In my daughter's youth and adolescence, she often cried four or five times a day about this or that until I was exhausted and frustrated. I knew she wanted something from me beyond whatever we argued about but didn't know what. In elementary school, the psychologist asked to meet with her on a regular basis because she so frequently asked teachers, *Is this right? Is it okay?* as though she couldn't tell where she stood in terms of performance. In middle school, she referred to a friend's friend as a *boyfriend*. Alarmed her friends had started dating so young, I asked if the boy was really a *boyfriend*. Ari wanted to know what that meant, and I said a friendship that eventually leads to a sexual relationship. After that, I never heard the word *boyfriend* again. When she did ask about my personal history regarding sex, I didn't tell her, saying when the time came for her to decide about becoming sexually active, she had to make up her own mind without being influenced by my experience. What I didn't tell her, but that she probably discerned, was that I didn't trust her to keep our conversations private. She never asked me anything private again.

In terms of my son, he'd always been an active kid. But after fifth grade, he just slowed down. Everything took twice as long to complete: walking to the park, doing chores, completing homework. His interest in school waned and his friend circle shrank. I took him to the doctor, who didn't find any obvious malady. I took him to a psychologist, who, after receiving the assessment responses from his teachers, diagnosed him with Attention Deficit Disorder, the form of ADHD that excludes hyperactivity. But I remember, too, ghostly voices, which might have been my own thoughts or the suggestions of my sisters or friends: *Could he be depressed?* I checked the symptoms of depression and they didn't seem to fit.

Didn't seem to.

I'm still haunted by the memory of him in sixth grade when he came to me one afternoon and said, "Remember you said I should ask if I needed help in school? I think I need help."

And I said, "Well you really wanted to do better on your own. You really pushed back on Dad and me to back off. That you'd take care of things. Let's see what you can do. This is your chance to take the lead."

I still can't believe I denied him help when he most needed it.

Upon remembering such shameful moments, my first reaction was to apologize to my kids. At this point, my daughter had graduated from college and lived in Oakland. My son was in junior college and still lived with us. I'd been sharing with them how my dad's undiagnosed autism may have affected me. One day my son was wandered into the kitchen while I was baking something.

When he sat to check his phone, I summoned my courage and said, "Hey."

He looked up.

"I know I've been telling you about all the stuff with Papa, what I've learned and everything," I said, referring to my dad by the nickname he chose over *Grandpa*. "But, I know it was hard on you and Ari. I mean, I'm sorry I wasn't as emotionally present as I could be. But I'm here now. You can, you know, share things with me."

He calmly looked at me and said, "I don't think so. You're not my emotional confidante."

Stunned to silence, stung to my core, I instantly knew what he said was true. His beautiful phrasing, if brutal, confirmed my suspicions. Simply attending to logistical parenting tasks and responsibilities does not guarantee you'll be emotionally close to your children.

I protected my daughter and son in the literal sense. Neither died nor got injured due to lack of vigilance. Both received regular healthcare, dental checkups, and close involvement in their education. Both had more than enough clothes to wear, a roof over their heads, two loving parents. Not to mention we had lots of good times. Days at the beach, birthday parties, summer visits to the East Coast. As a family, we backpacked in Northern California and went to Hawaii. My husband and I watched our kids play sports: water polo, basketball, baseball, soccer.

But that's the thing.

You can cheer for them during hundreds of sporting events. You can shower them with gifts. You can travel them around the world. You can spend years telling them you love them. But if you miss their first attempts to talk to you about what matters most to them—their worries, fears and delights—they'll separate from you emotionally until they come to think of you as nothing more than a friendly store clerk. Someone to smile at and treat with basic courtesy, but who disappears from their mind the moment you're out of sight. They're fond of you. They may even feel obligated to observe certain formalities, such as calling on your birthday. But if they come in to buy something and you suddenly want to know how they feel at a deep level, they look at you as my son looked at me. *I appreciate your concern, but you're not the person with whom I share.*

The way I had looked at my mom and dad.

To survive the damage I incurred as a kid, I enfolded myself in the costume of a *good mom*, a part I played well and believed to be genuine. I didn't know yet how I lied to myself and everyone else about who I was and how I felt about anything. I didn't know yet I had emotionally shut down when only a kid of two or three. I couldn't feel the wall that separated me from my kids, of, *You're over there and I'm here*, rather than, *We're all here together and I'm here for you.*

But my kids did.

They knew I was holding back. They reached for me and pleaded with me to share myself in the way of kids who feel deeply, but as yet have no words for what they want or need.

And what did I do? I hugged them but never let them pass my internal *No Trespassing* sign, so that my embrace equated to a hard pat on the back.

As my frustrated adolescent daughter once yelled at me, "You never tell me anything." By which she meant I never told her anything personal that might make me vulnerable, and in turn, invite her to be vulnerable with me.

When you hurt your own kids to such a deep degree—when you emotionally shut them out—you don't get do-overs.

Not even if you didn't mean to.

Not even if you were unaware of what you were doing.

Not even if you'd simply and unwittingly modeled the behavior you received.

Your parents unintentionally maimed you, and then you turned around and injured your kids in a similar way. When you finally wake up to see what you've done, you tell your kids you'll do anything—*anything*—to take back what you did. Lay down in front of an oncoming train. Give away your life savings. Plead on your knees. Explain and explain and explain.

But it's too late.

It's too fucking late.

The bitterness I felt acted like poison that kept me alive just enough to experience an agony without end as every nerve screamed from a mouth that never opened.

By now I was far down that dark, isolated, treacherous road. I had no tools to deal with my guilt, much less those to treat myself with kindness. I couldn't see the good things I'd done for my kids, like instilling a love of art and the need to be kind to others. I couldn't see how my angst had become overexaggerated. I didn't have anyone to confide in other than my husband, who said I was being too hard on myself.

Which brings me to the pity party.

Part VII
Healing

Vulnerability

It's not natural to bare
your breast,

to, with unarmed fingertips, pull
away

the scant material barricading
the pump that is your life.

To make a close-range target for someone

to shoot at
to laugh at
to do nothing about

in the off chance the person—

the people
the world

—will empathize and

pity you
like you a little
love you.

Try unclothing yourself even once
and eyes roll, your death predicted,

when the opposite is true.

Look at me.

I mean really. Look
this way,
at me.

Watch as I lift my nude
fingers, hot with touch.

Study how they curve and hook to the edge
of my cheap cotton tank top,

pulling the fabric away
for you to see

the freckle on my left breast
the white of my skin, and beneath,
the faint blue threads, like gun smoke drifting upward.

I appear

weak
undignified
not dangerous.

But I am,
to you

who stands close
who is unsuspecting
who does not realize

nakedness means there's nothing
else to offer, to lose.

I can, if I want, strangle
with my truth

either

killing
or birthing

us both.

Mike retired in April 2014, two years after Mom died. He hadn't been back to St. Louis in a while, and so he went to visit his mom for two weeks.

He left on a Thursday. When I woke on Friday, I remained in bed, alone in a quiet house. I listened to the fan on our dresser, the hum of the refrigerator, birds singing.

I ate breakfast in the quiet. I cleaned my house in the quiet. I read and napped and woke again to quiet.

And all day in that quiet, I allowed myself to absorb the truth.

I'd been injured.

—

All of my life I'd been taught by religion and culture to:

Stop feeling sorry for yourself.

Be grateful for what you've got.

There are so many others who are so much worse off than you.

How sadly true that some people get squashed by the actions of others. Those defrauded of their life savings. Children traumatized by physical and verbal abuse. Believers manipulated or molested by religious leaders or coaches. Citizens poisoned by legislators who vote against safety regulations. Those flooded by faulty dams built by companies trying to cut corners. Add to that the survivors of murder, genocide, starvation, human slavery and the long list of other human atrocities.

On the flip side are situations where no one is to blame. People who have mental health issues, hereditary conditions, or cancer and other illnesses. People who struggle through life undiagnosed because they don't have the resources to get care, or because scientists and doctors haven't yet named the malady or its underlying cause. Those who do the best they can with what they're given. Parents who try to do right by their children and give them more opportunities than they were given.

People who keep their children fed, clothed, and housed and who try to show them a good time.

Good people with good hearts and good intentions, who simply missed something important.

Like my parents.

Like me.

When no blame can be assigned, the societal message is doubly clear: we don't have the right to feel bad.

Yet we do.

That leaves us in an emotional quandary. We hurt but don't feel we can complain. The timeworn method for solving the problem is to bury the angst. Maybe that works for some of us. But my suspicion is, while we claim that's true, small but persistent unhappiness continues to plague us, pricking us over and over as a means of waking us to the fact there's still something very wrong. A pain, an infection, a wound that promises to worsen and causes us to act badly toward others, even when that's not what we want or intend.

During my day of quiet, I finally realized that a *chin up!* state of denial does no one any good. So for the first time, I resisted the urge to label myself as an ungrateful whiner and instead thought, *Fuck that. I'm sad. I get to be sad. My dad and mom hurt me. They didn't mean to, but that's what happened.*

I wondered if I should cancel dinner with two friends and stay amidst the quiet. But I didn't. I baked a dessert and went to dinner. When they asked how I was, this time I didn't say, *Fine!* I told them about my day, about my hurt, and they felt bad with me. Because I allowed myself to be vulnerable with them, they shared how they suffered, too, and we all felt bad together. But we felt good letting the hurt out. As we talked, I remember gazing from one friend to the other while thinking with wonder, *So this is what it's like to be truthful about myself. So this is what it's like to share myself with others instead of pretending everything is fine.*

—

In my long-time critique group, we follow the pattern of having two people submit segments of their writing before a meeting. Those of us not submitting read the pieces, then come to the meeting and offer suggestions for improvement. Everyone is intelligent, skilled and motivated to support and help. Everyone argues the merits for various adjustments. Anyone watching us would think we're enthusiastic accountants talking fascinating changes to the tax code.

While most times I come away energized and understanding what I need to do to improve, other times I feel gutted at failing so miserably to convey stories that grow from the tenderest places within me.

After such meetings, I take refuge in sleep, only to wake with a long, loud groan and the spiritual equivalent of a splitting head-ache. I spend the day alternately angry the universe can't see the obvious brilliance in my work, after which I wallow in deep wells of pity before falling into bed, a wreck. I'm exaggerating, but only a little.

When I wake up, the pity is gone. The comments people made have circulated long enough I now see the beauty of those ideas. Even better, the suggestions give me a path forward, and soon my mind focuses on implementing the changes. The pity party over, I set to work.

I include the notion of a pity party in my *Growing Great Characters From the Ground Up* book under the title *The Day-After-A-Critique Hangover*. Since writing that book, the belief has only grown stronger over the years that no advancement can be made before taking that first step: acknowledging how bummed out we feel.

So instead of denying ourselves the right to feel sad, which keeps the pain close and fresh, why not throw ourselves a cry-fest? A real Festival of Whine. An occasion dedicated to blubbering our hearts out and scrawling terrible things in diaries no one will ever see. An occasion where we blab with no thought for sounding ungrateful, and during which we describe in detail the injury we suffered. When finished gorging on our angst and vomiting out the excess, we finally pass out.

Then we wake up. While we may not be refreshed, we're ready to take a shower, brush our teeth and move on.

After my day of quiet, the time had come to get to work.

turbulent flow

when she pours
the frothing
white
milk

into a clear
glass of
crystal
ice

and black
espresso,

the white light-
ning

jags downward
exploding the
darkness,

the annihilation

brutal

total

indifferent

and suddenly—
done

the new order
not black
not white

but a light
brown

all before my lips
can utter,
Wow.

Turbulent flow,
she says,

my dark
eyes
lift

to hers, of
light
blue

Turbulent flow,

she says again
in the same
low tone

in which she
spoke

her name
the first
time

she poured
her hand
into
mine

Solving problems means first examining what went wrong.

In my case, one of my most significant problems was unintentionally adopting the poor communication habits of an undiagnosed ASD person.

But first I'd like to start by listing the skills Dad gave me that have proven instrumental in my life. He helped me develop a fantastic work ethic. He also taught me to save money, which is a cornerstone of survival. He encouraged me to think independently by collecting facts from multiple reputable sources before making decisions or forming opinions, rather than falling prey to emotional manipulation, which has protected me from scammers and rampant disinformation on everything from fitness miracle cures to conspiracy theories. He demonstrated the discipline for, and necessity of, daily physical activity as a means of keeping the mind and body sharp and mental health intact. He behaved in a manner that bespoke his internal belief we should be kind to everyone, no matter their ethnicity, race, religion or socio-economic status. He was a righteous dude in many ways.

Not surprisingly, his social skills left me with habits I've had to overcome. The first concept I needed to override was the belief that every social interaction should have a point, otherwise it was a waste of time. That's why he didn't understand *hanging out*. Nor did I, except with my sisters. By only socializing during specific activities or leaving just as people started to unwind, I most likely gave them the impression I didn't care about them, or worse, they bored me. I've since learned relaxing with others creates an atmosphere in which people feel comfortable sharing.

Dad also gave the impression that if people gift you something, you gift them something of equal or greater value, and sooner rather than later so you're not in their debt. The idea people will give you anything because it makes them feel good or to express their appreciation of you is crazy because everyone knows you're not valuable.

A third lesson was that you don't ask for help unless you really, really, really need it. You don't add to people's burdens by bothering them with your problems. Rather than complain, only speak up when you have something edifying to say. And don't waste time trying to figure out the source of your upset when there are more important obligations to fulfill.

Once aware of the social habits that might be stymying my ability to connect with others, I realized I couldn't repair my relationship with my kids until I first fixed my communication problems. But how would I, a person without a vocabulary for expressing my emotions, develop a pathway to better communication, especially involving issues that were so hard to explain?

—

In the late 1980s, Mike and I moved to Madison, WI, so he could get his master's degree in computer science. I got a job at a daily newspaper. Lowest on the newsroom totem pole, I got assigned the geriatric beat. Besides putting together a calendar of senior events that included free podiatry care clinics and euchre tournaments, I had the chance to write features about events that interested me.

For one article, I enrolled in a women's self-defense class held in a big two-story house that had been turned into a community center. One of a dozen women, I sat in a circle on the wood floor and listened to the instructor, a thin, short-haired woman in her thirties.

At one point she said, "Now let's all get up. We have to practice yelling."

The idea surprised me because we obviously knew how to yell, and of course would do so in a life-threatening moment. But I got to my feet.

The instructor stood like the rest of us, with arms at her sides. "When we're in a moment of danger, the last thing we want to do is scream. Screaming scares people and doesn't tell them anything about what's going on. I mean, what does 'Ahhhh!' mean?"

Some women laughed.

Smiling, the instructor said, "Instead, what we want to do is yell a clear message that tells people what action to take, which if we're attacked is to call the police. The problem is that when our adrenaline is through the roof, we don't think clearly and we don't have time to search around for what to say. So we're tongue-tied and resort to screaming. That's why we've got to have our message ready ahead of time. Something simple and clear. Anybody have an idea of what we should say?"

"'Rape,'" said an older woman to my left.

Expressions around the room ranged from grimaces to cynical smiles that acknowledged the common threat of assault all women face.

The instructor said, "Unfortunately, that word scares people and could deter them from helping."

A few mouths popped open. Some women glanced around. Everyone looked shocked.

"That's outrageous," said the older woman near me. "If I yell 'Rape!' no one will come help?"

The instructor nodded.

"So what are we supposed to say?" said a petite young woman.

"'Fire!'" the instructor said. "But the thing is, we have to practice yelling 'Fire!' loud enough to get people's attention. Not many of us yell on a regular basis, and hopefully none of us has been in a live-or-die situation where we've had to yell. But that means we're inexperienced. We think we'll yell, but we might get choked up by fear. That's why we've got to practice, so in a chaotic moment, our minds remember what to say and how loud to say it. So that's what we're going to do now. I'll count to three and you'll yell 'Fire!' loud as you can. Remind yourselves of the circumstances. Someone is threatening you. You're yelling to save your life. Okay?"

We nodded.

"One, two, three—"

We yelled.

The sound we made was no louder or fiercer than if we were yelling *hello* to a friend across a parking lot. We stood in silence looking at one another, appalled at how right the instructor had been in predicting our tepid response. Though we'd been told our lives might be at stake, we'd been unable to escape our gender role of being polite, non-confrontational and quiet.

The instructor studied us, her eyes steady. "That's why we practice. We think when the time comes to save ourselves, we'll have the words and the will, and we might have both of those. But we females are raised to be docile. To not make too much noise. To be polite. Look at how we stand."

We glanced at one another.

"Arms at our sides," the instructor said, "making ourselves small as possible. Signaling we're the opposite of dangerous. That we'll acquiesce. In threatening situations, all of that cultural baggage works against us. So. We're going to do this again. This time, everyone take two steps back."

We did and our circle expanded.

"Now, think how you act when someone surprises you," and the instructor dropped into a wide-legged crouch, hands up, eyes wide. We did the same, now finally serious about our survival and no longer caring if we looked weird. Where before I was an impartial observer, concentrating on the others and their reactions, I became a full participant. My mind combined the scary incidents I'd experienced and first-hand accounts of assaults against women I knew. By the expressions on my classmates' faces, they, too, seemed to be recalling aggressions committed in dark alleys, empty office buildings, late-night college campuses, or dorm rooms.

"We instantly know we're under attack," the instructor said. "Instead of dismissing the notion that we're overreacting, which is what we're taught to think, we embrace our gut reaction that someone is trying to hurt us. This is our life we're talking about. Our life! Others don't have the right to tell us we're making too much of a fuss. Others don't get to abuse us. Now. One, two, three—"

"Fire!" we yelled, our mouths wide and fingers curled like claws, the veins in our necks thick with fast-moving blood.

"Again!"

"Fire!"

"And again!"

"Fire!"

And I understood then what I hadn't before. Communicating well isn't just about saying the right words at the right time in the right way. It's about imagining and preparing for those opportunities so that when they arrive, you seize them.

Now so many years later, I realized I lacked not only the words necessary to connect with others, but practice in speaking those words and watching for opportunities to do so.

For example:

Seven years after Mom died, my daughter and I took a hike. On the way home, we started discussing the topic of beauty, and suddenly her voice took on an edge of anger. I tried to clarify my point as we parked and walked into her apartment, but everything I said seemed to confirm an opinion she found personally insulting. Just as we were about to enter her apartment, she said, "I can't talk about this anymore."

We walked in to find her fiancé and my son playing on their computers. Her fiancé asked if I'd be staying to dinner, and I said, "I don't know. I upset Ari."

He said, "Uh-oh," and kept playing his game.

Ari went to change. The men played their games. I just stood there, feeling confused, misunderstood and angry. But I didn't want to speak up, to make a fuss, to be the source of drama. If I did, I'd once again be the Bad Mom who acted like a spoiled adolescent.

Ari came out showered, dressed and apparently fine. Her ability to drop the subject after accusing me of being insensitive made me boil hotter. Why didn't she, or any of them, see I was miserable? Why didn't they help by asking me, *Do you want to talk about it?* Because I would have said, *Yes! Please! What went wrong and how do we fix it?*

My son and daughter did ask if I was all right, but that's not the same question. How did they expect me to respond? What words would keep me from looking like the Wicked Witch of the West? So I said nothing. I tried to calm down and agreed to watch a movie, during which my anger and confusion continued to build. When the movie ended, I couldn't take feeling like such a failure anymore. I told my son we had to leave and I left without hugging my daughter, which even now feels like a childish, unforgivable act. But in that moment, I couldn't pretend love and warmth.

I was so angry and hurt I couldn't talk all the way home and so missed the opportunity to catch up with my son, who was visiting from where he lived in Los Angeles.

Not surprisingly, I didn't sleep well that night. But during that tumultuous tossing and turning, an important piece of my life puzzle fell into place. As a little kid, I at some point determined I couldn't trust my mother with my innermost feelings. Once I cut her out of my emotional loop, she had no way to learn who I was or what I needed besides the obvious. Sometimes when she asked a question, the question itself revealed how little she knew about me. Unable to believe she could be so dumb, I gave her a snippy reply. What I failed to realize was that I kept her dumb.

The next day, I sent my daughter a letter explaining my epiphany, with the adage, "And that, I suspect, is what happened between you and me. I'd like to change that."

Changing a negative dynamic isn't easy because you're asking the person to trust you in an area of life where you've been untrustworthy. Not surprisingly, my daughter responded kindly and honestly but kept to a polite distance. But at least I made a start. From there, I began talking more with my son, who fortunately has an affinity for talking about personal relationships. At some point, I mentioned the incident at the apartment.

Then I asked, "How come you two didn't ask if I wanted to talk about what happened?"

He looked at me, incredulous. "We did! Several times. You said you were fine, even though you didn't look fine. You clearly didn't want to talk about it."

Only then did I realize both he and Ari had opened doors for discussion. Not only had I been oblivious to those opportunities, but had I wanted to take them, I wouldn't have had the words to speak.

I didn't have the words to tell people what they needed to know. To understand me. To help me. Instead, I silently endured whatever hurtful incident occurred—a tart reply, exclusion from an activity, etc.—after which my pain would leak out in passive-aggressive ways that caused confusion and strife for myself and those around me.

Now that the pity party was over, I knew my wish to communicate better required a Poor-Communication Eradication Plan.

Then I'd have to practice.

And practice.

And practice.

But *that* I knew how to do.

–

I got married the day after I graduated college in 1986. My husband and I lived in St. Louis, where I began freelancing for area papers. I also started teaching senior fitness classes at a YMCA. From then on, no matter what full-time job I had, I taught aerobics or strength classes as a side gig. When my kids were in middle school, and I already had a few books published, I became a full-time personal trainer and fitness instructor.

When clients tell me about physical problems, the first step is to rule out serious issues by having them consult a doctor, and if need be, get an X-ray, MRI or both. If the problem appears to be more minor and due to a muscular imbalance or poor form, I teach them a four-step process for eliminating the problem: take an educated guess about the source, devise a way to test the theory, carry out the experiment over the course of a few days or weeks, and analyze the results. If the discomfort goes away for good, we can safely assume we found and corrected the problem. If the issue persists, we start the process again with the next-best guess.

Often a problem arises from something very small, like not pressing down on the big toes properly, which can destabilize the knee. Correcting the problem can be equally as easy, and in this case would involve consistently pressuring the big toes when doing activities. If people focus on implementing the solution, their effort can lead to significant change almost immediately or within a relatively short period of time. People are often surprised that by finding and acknowledging the source of the issue and making small but important changes, they can quickly rid themselves of pain that's dogged them for months or years.

I reasoned if the process worked for the body, maybe it would work for repairing the heart.

–

I made a checklist of what I wanted to accomplish:
to be honest with myself and others rather than hide behind the lie of *I'm fine.*
to turn internal me into public me by allowing others to see my passions and imperfections.
to truly connect with others by letting them know I care about them and allowing them to care about me.
lastly, I didn't want to feel guilty anymore about the parenting errors I made.

I found the second therapist and sent her my list. We got to work.

Initially, learning to be more honest felt like torture. When someone asked how I felt about anything—even something small and unimportant—I had to physically close my lips tight against the immediate response of *Fine!* Then as the person waited, clearly wondering why I needed so long to reply, I forced myself away from the response I thought they wanted to hear and that would be most convenient for everyone and asked myself how I truly felt. When the answer came, I had to convince myself I had a right to feel as I did. Then I forced myself to open my mouth and actually speak the words without anger, insult or any other emotional edge. They'd been polite in asking for my input, which meant they deserved a similar reply.

I know I normally agree to split the Moo Shu shrimp, but eating half leaves me hungry and you have a whole other entree you ordered to fill you up, so I'd like my own order. Or let's get two orders and have some for leftovers.

I feel off today. I think it's partly because my conversation with ___ really worried me. He says he's doing okay, but that doesn't seem like the case.

I feel like I should go biking, but it's so cold outside and I'm feeling worn out. I really just want to do yoga in a nice, warm room. Yeah, that's what I'm going to do.

Within a month of persistent practice, symptom one vanished.

When trying to reduce my sense of isolation, the therapist told me everyone has a secret inner life. I knew that in theory, but by talking with her, realized I had a ratio problem. If the internal me felt completely secret, and the external me felt like a lie, that made a ratio of 10:0. I had to reduce the former and increase the latter.

By finally understanding the problem, I was able to see the cause. As a nobody, I didn't feel I had the right to burden anyone with my thoughts and emotions. For years I packed my mind with what had seemed like top-secret intel, only to realize most of the information consisted of stupid little secrets.

I began to dispose of one secret at a time by dropping the nugget into a conversation. Astonishingly enough, what I'd considered so terribly important was not. Either nobody cared or they found the information useful and told me how my experience was similar to something they'd gone through. Clearing away such emotional clutter led to immediate and enormous relief that left me feeling light, free and able to breathe.

I definitely had an eating disorder when I was a kid, which would have grown into full-blown binging if I hadn't hated throwing up so much.

And the world didn't collapse.

I don't really have a relationship with my dad.

And no one swooned.

It hurts when you say things like that.

And people listened.

Symptom two vanished.

Learning to connect with others proved a more difficult task. I'd grown used to comforting and supporting others. That made me feel good about myself but also allowed me to hide which led to feeling lonely.

On my fifty-fifth birthday, that changed.

While my husband and I often go to dinner at local places we both enjoy, he's not only intellectually allergic to hoity-toity but has a palate oriented toward the likes of Steak 'n Shake. I, on the other hand, enjoy the occasional fancy culinary adventure. So for my birthday, I went to dinner with my daughter and her fiancé and his family at a cool bistro in the Mission District of San Francisco. We sat outside on a mild evening and watched people go by as the sun moved toward dusk. Delicious aromas from the kitchen escaped when waiters came out carrying food. We delighted in the flavors of every unusual dish.

As I looked around at those at my table—some talking, others chewing, all distracted and busy with the business of being together—for the first time I didn't feel alone. These people came to be with imperfect me, who no longer played a role. My smile felt true. My interest in everyone felt sincere. And when they picked up the tab before I could, rather than feel I'd somehow bamboozled them into treating me better than I deserved, I felt loved.

Symptom three—

Gone.

—

Getting rid of guilt proved a tougher uphill road that didn't follow an efficient, linear path.

Eager to apologize to my kids, I pursued both of them for opportunities to bare my soul and finish up with all of this time-consuming self-correction. But such neediness proves to be a burden to others. The more you pursue them, the faster they run. That seemed true for my daughter.

My son suggested that rather than text her or keep suggesting activities, I should wait until she came to me. This would be a practical application of the metaphorical test, *If you love them, set them free. If they come back, they're yours. If they don't, they never were.*

In the two weeks I didn't call my daughter, she texted and called her dad multiple times. Hurt, angry and impatient, I waited. Then she called. We talked for a while and our conversation felt easy. Again I didn't hear from her for a while. And again, she called.

In turn, my philosopher son now levels with me regularly and calls me out when I obliquely hint at qualms, rather than stating my problem clearly. While emotionally exhausting sometimes, the process has led to a deeper understanding between us.

That said, I won't paint you a rosy picture as my mom might have. I experienced many setbacks when attempting to correct past wrongs and rid myself of guilt. Sometimes I took the easy way out of *I'm fine!* rather than hassle with a complicated explanation. Sometimes a passive-aggressive comment slipped out. After such a stumble, I wrote about the incident in a journal, which helped me think through my behavior and thoughts. Slowly, I gained the strength and confidence to face people and either apologize or clarify.

And I do mean *slowly*. At one point, I thought I'd never get rid of my guilt. That no matter how much I wanted my kids to give me another chance, if I didn't support them when they needed me most, I'd never have the honor of being needed by them in a significant way.

Though harsh, the thought led me to the first of two key epiphanies: I had to stop looking to other people to fix me and instead concentrate on fixing myself.

The second epiphany came from my current therapist, who said when we linger in guilt, we fail to acknowledge the ability of others to overcome the hardship.

When I told my sister, Dee, she said, "Ain't that the truth. The only thing you can do is tell people you made a mistake and there's absolutely nothing you could have done to keep from making that mistake. And now here we are and we've all got to deal with it."

—

Fixing myself meant learning to be kind to myself, a solution that didn't occur to me until I listened to a podcast that featured Kristin Neff, an associate professor of educational psychology at the University of Texas at Austin. Author of *Self-Compassion:*

The Proven Power of Being Kind to Yourself, she maintains the self-compassion.org website. I got the book, read the first chapter, followed the exercises and wrote down my thoughts. I went to therapy and talked about what I learned, a process that led to the monumental discovery of how badly I treated myself. As in:

you're stupid.

you're a rotten mom.

stop being so selfish and needy.

To get away from my tyrant self, I bought index cards and wrote down moments in which I made an error but rather than degrade myself, I learned to be kind.

Today when riding with a biking friend and he asked me to go to coffee afterward, my inner critic didn't pipe up to tell me I should bow out, that I was boring and how awkward when he learned that. Instead, I thought, Why not? I went and didn't feel like just me isn't enough.

The kinder I became to myself, and the farther I got from that dark self-loathing, the better I could see how others around me—and particularly women—had the same tendency to be far nicer to everyone other than themselves.

That "black goo" of negativity, as Professor Neff calls it, keeps us in a dark limbo. "When we feel fatally flawed, incapable of handling the challenges life throws our way, we tend to shut down emotionally in response to fear and shame."

Only by holding my own hand and reminding myself I'm a good person who wants to be a better person could I bear to do what I'd avoided: keep the focus on me long enough to finally understand why I sometimes acted in negative ways that caused unhappiness.

I continued to practice self-kindness. I learned to set boundaries, which I'd never done because the concept didn't exist in my youth. I came to understand any harm I caused my kids stemmed from the depth of my own impairment. I cried long and hard about that truth and discovered crying is healthy.

Once I could clearly see how many potholes marred my journey, I felt heady with vindication. I wasn't a rotten, stupid person after all.

Parenting

People think when swimming, when submerged, you're surrounded by silence. Blame movies. Those slo-mo shots of bodies curved as poetry, every exhale a string of pearls suspended in blue. When really, once immersed, the water roars. Arms pinwheel a lung-burning churn. Fish mouth gropes for a slice of air. The world of you, and around you, froths, obscuring hazards caught just in time, or not. Before jumping in, you only sensed the potential for disquiet. Now in, the explosion of sound and motion makes clear the only thing between you and belly up is a pocket of fast-disappearing air deep inside you, a buoyancy with a time limit. To *sink*, to *swim*, not a choice. You swim. And sink. And swim. And sink. Until you grab the wall. Water pulls away from your face, dragging with it who you thought you were. Your eyes and mouth stretch open as they had not before and to a degree that hurts. And though your lungs refill and your womb quiets, and though the water stills, the life-giving, life taking-away liquid gently circles your throat, holding you, as it always will. And someone asks, *Did you have a nice swim?*

Seven years after Mom died, I signed a contract with Vine Leaves Press to publish my second novel *Winter Light*. Having had two previous books published, I knew marketing the book would require crawling out of my self-induced shell.

When my writing book was published thirteen years previous, my kids were young and my household busy with their activities. I was teaching fitness classes and personal training, providing developmental editing for writing clients, and offering writing workshops for writing clubs and conferences. Social media and tech marketing had just begun to replace the old methods of handing out paper flyers and keeping an email list in a Word document rather than using automation. A few years later my novel, *The Wind Thief,* was published. The more I promoted, the more shine I applied to my exterior to cover my nothing-who-knows-nothing interior. Rather than bring me closer to people, I pulled back further and felt exhausted from trying to hide so much and act so perfectly.

Then I began pitching my next book to agents. I failed. I stopped writing and fell down the rabbit hole for the next eight years.

I emerged. I learned honesty. I learned I was loved.

When I got the contract and committed to marketing *Winter Light*, I reopened my social media, and unlike the previous time, felt joyful about reconnecting with others because I had finally learned how to be authentic.

When younger, I would have scoffed at that word, *authentic*, as so much emotional mumbo-jumbo. I now know the term simply means admitting you're human. I regularly confess my errors to people who then smile and welcome me into the fold. And instead of focusing my attention inward and worrying about who will find out about impostor me, I turn my attention outward, toward what's happening in others' lives: vacations, anniversaries, deaths, delicious meals, beloved pets. I delight in catching up with people I've known for a long time. When I find myself putting an extra layer of polish on a social media post, I tell myself, *Who are you kidding? Fess up, girl!* And I pin up my dirty laundry for all to see, the ugliness fading day by day as the humor grows brighter.

I've made friends and friends and friends. Friends I bike with and artists whose work I love. I cook with foodies more talented than myself and read the books of writer friends. I surf with buddies who follow the tides. It's clear I've learned the skill of hanging out.

I don't think anymore about needing to hide my emptiness because I don't feel empty. I am what I am and offer what I can. The shine of the people in my life fills me. When I'm down, I admit that to my husband, my kids, my friends. Then I go surfing or biking and feel better. When I'm feeling happy, which is most of the time, I cast my gaze toward the cool things happening around me and encourage that momentum. On depressing days, I acknowledge the negative and push hard toward the positive.

Perfection it ain't. But at least I no longer pretend the impossible.

I still meet people in-person or online from that time of pre-enlightenment who treat me with a coolness that reflects my former self who kept others at a polite distance and dropped friendships because I couldn't imagine people might actually like me. People who must have felt hurt and disappointed by the apparently cold, shallow behavior of someone who initially seemed sincere, yet turned out to be fake. And I don't blame them. If that's what you remember about a person, that's what you remember.

But at least I no longer live in that version of myself.

—

From what I've written, you can see my journey was far from smooth, but instead resembled that crazy road trip my dad experienced with his family. Without a map or working GPS, I drove on badly maintained roads, got lost, backed up, took a new route and repeated all of that again and again, while each time hoping I'd get closer to my destination.

Now for the pep talk.

Part VIII
Bliss

Eudaimonea: a Greek word referring to a state of having a good indwelling spirit or being in a contented state of health, happiness and prosperity; "human flourishing" has been proposed as a more accurate translation.

Etymologically, it consists of the words "eu" ("good") and "daimōn" ("spirit").

Eudaimonea

As the summer sun
went down, my
son and I sat
outside

on a hard bench
of a Cuban restaurant
along an ugly LA
street

the day before I left
and he stayed

in his new
life.

His girlfriend, her
parents, all of us eating

when he leaned
his shoulder against me

and I released into
him

a moment

as the brilliant sun
went down
in a hazy sky

Every family is a collection of banged-up psyches. Why not just accept that reality rather than embark on the long, rough road of self-improvement?

Why hang out our dirty laundry?

Why make a fuss?

Why stir the pot?

Why seek to learn unsavory truths about ourselves?

Why spend money on therapy when we could fund a vacation?

Why insist something is wrong when everything else is mostly right?

Why be a pain to everyone around us while attempting to put together a puzzle that'll never be complete?

The answer is simple: to live a happier life.

I drove down that shadowy road because I didn't want to be just okay, as in *sort of all right* or *mostly fine*. I want to be happy now and for as much of my earthly time as possible. And not just happy, but blissful. Happy to the highest possible level so that when I near death, I'm so exhausted by the joy, desperation, humor, worry and love that defines a human life, I'm more than ready for lights out.

So I agonized and gnashed my teeth and lost weight. I wrote angry things in my journal and acted badly despite trying not to. I apologized ad nauseam to everyone around me. For being spacey. For being moody. For having hurt them.

But then.

I saw the worst.

I knew the worst.

I really did find a sea serpent. But the scaly, snaky, sharp-toothed water dragon didn't turn out to be my dad, or any one person, but instead the damage I incurred by virtue of being me. The unique combination of my personality, brain, preferences, experiences and position within my family caused me to respond as I did to a challenge that met me at birth.

If you've gotten to a point where life keeps stabbing you in the heart—the loss of important relationships, loneliness, habits that distance you from others—maybe it's your time to start down that road. If you do, expect to hurt. And know there's no guarantee you'll find that elusive beast that's souring your life. But the chance of discovering the demon is literally a hundred percent higher than doing nothing. Trying is what matters most.

As Jody Smith concluded in her 2015 article, "The feeling of invisibility and of having no voice, the fear of rocking the boat or of being called selfish for talking about yourself and how you feel may be deeply ingrained. It may be your first and biggest obstacle. But if you can climb over that one, and continue to climb over it, you may find it was your only real obstacle."

—

While deciding to start a journey can be the most difficult step, the second is knowing where to start. Consider first talking to yourself by writing in a journal, drawing a picture, making a voice memo or writing a song or poem. Whatever the medium, open a self-dialogue to help you find the shape and feel of your unhappiness and define the occasions and relationships that feel wrong. Then take your observations to a psychotherapist or psychiatrist. Read self-help books or sign up for self-help programs that offer insight into what you've observed and that will put you in touch with your feelings. Talk to family members, friends or those in a support group.

Be aware that at the beginning, whatever you say will sound like so much whining and complaining. But if you set a consistent pace, then push, persevere, limp, trudge and march onward, ever onward, past one mind-blowing insight after another, you'll begin to notice the symptoms of unhappiness disappear. The nervous stomach will abate. The feeling of isolation will lessen. Thoughts of self-harm will diminish to a point where you understand their danger, and if necessary, get professional help. The length of time between unhappy moments will stretch so that when they occur, they're jarring enough to help you self-correct. You'll get better at not only sharing what you feel but also doing so in a more positive manner. That will draw closer those who love and support you. You'll have more energy to help them in return. The dead carcass of *life isn't fair* will fall away as you grieve for both what happened and what didn't. You'll take responsibility for what you can change.

You'll pick up tools to help you in the future, like learning to apologize in a sincere and unequivocal way, as in *I was wrong,* rather than, *I was wrong, but* ... Sometimes those few sincerely-spoken, deeply-felt words can clear a life-long roadblock between you and the people you love. The obstruction gone, you can finally reach your destination, the peace that comes from fully understanding what happened.

As in:

My dad may have had an undiagnosed neurological condition that affected my self-esteem and communication system at an early age. There was no way he or my mom could have known the possible psychological ramifications on us kids. My survival methods proved effective but harmful in the long run.

The more I thought about my parents while writing this book—their upbringing, inherent natures, genetic makeup, emotional vulnerabilities, what stressed them, what scared them, what shamed them—my anger seeped away. By understanding their demons, I finally understood they, like all of us do, took actions—both good and bad—to survive the challenges they faced.

My thinking continued to evolve until I finally viewed them not as two adults, not as my parents, not as a married couple, but rather as just two people. Only then did I see how we were all alike.

For example.

–

One of the first vacations I remember as a kid was when my family drove to a cabin campground on Houghton Lake in Michigan. For a week, we occupied one of a dozen cabins built around a central playground with a path leading to a sandy beach on the lake. From the moment we parked amid the pine trees, I could feel the freedom this safe little universe afforded me and my sisters. Absent traffic, scary strangers and everyday responsibilities, we kids could have fun all day with little parental supervision. My spirit swelled into muscled, sun-baked joy as I ran with my sisters and the other kids who'd come with their families.

I've since thought back on that youthful joy and imagined my mom and dad not as parents, but as two kids in our campground gang during that magical time.

About my age of seven years old, Norma is a little shy, but her smile invites complete trust. She'll never make fun of you behind your back. Though a little skittish, and too plump to do the monkey bars, her imagination is topnotch and she's willing to push me on the swing until I can pump myself high. I like that she's always a little sweaty, like me, and her curly hair escapes her ponytail holder. She doesn't worry about looking perfect.

About the same age, Ray is fun, too, if a little weird. He's eager to do everything and wants to make all the rules, but we ignore him and he eventually follows or goes off to do his own thing. He's not a bully who will smile then push you down. He has light brown hair and his eyes match the sky.

Norma and Ray and the other campground kids play tag with my sisters and me. We dodge around the merry-go-round, trying to escape the person who's *it*. We swim in the lake and Norma has a one-piece bathing suit made of material with big pink flowers. She doesn't like to get her head wet, though, and has to hold her nose when she goes under. All of us dig for worms at the lake edge and in the grass after it rains. We store them in little Styrofoam cups of dirt then find an adult willing to row us out onto the lake to reel in fish for the Friday Night Fish Fry. In the evening we all leap about, catching lightning bugs that firework the darkening sky. We're careful to cup our hands so we don't smush the bugs, which are gentle and beautiful, like little fairies.

Sometimes, when I want to be alone, I'll swing on the swing set. Sometimes, I see Norma reading on the front porch of her family's cabin. Sometimes, I see Ray pushing the merry-go-round in a fast circle before leaping on and laughing at the dizzying speed.

He, Norma, my sisters, me and the other kids: we all look at one another with bright eyes, excited by what we imagine life will be. We're sunburned, mosquito-bitten, usually hungry from racing around, and sometimes tired and irritable for the same reason. Yet we're more or less happy. None of us sees the trouble we're headed for. None of us knows, or can know, how we'll react when we get there. None of us has the intention of harming anyone and would be horrified to know such a thing could be true.

We're all friends, and I, like them, understand what we don't yet know how to say.

We're all doing the best we can.

—

That's what I hope for you.

That you take the nebulous journey, reach the top of the hill and cross the treacherous, heavily-shaded road. If you do, don't just pat yourself on the back. Give yourself a hearty pounding because you had the courage to face your worst fear.

And you killed that beast dead.

Now I'm less stressed and more sure. I deal with others in a truthful, more generous manner, a sincerity friends and family sense and return. No longer buried within myself, I look at the world through less selfish eyes and am more amazed than ever by the beauty I see, despite the bad things that happened along the way or will happen. I take myself less seriously, laugh more often and am no longer overly-sensitive. I'm regularly stunned by the people who really care about me and can better spot opportunities to help them in return.

Now parked atop Bliss Road, I step from the dark shade into the sunshine. I gaze across the rolling green land. Rather than be an unreachable dream, the hills are real and filled with birds, animals and walking paths. The clean air smells of oak and pine. The sun glints on the lake where my sister, Dee, and I just finished kayaking. She's in the winery behind me, buying a chilled bottle of white that will go well with grilled chicken and veggies and the lingering heat of a summer evening. After walking through the landscaped grounds, we'll drive home to her house where my other sister, the husbands and the now-grown kids have been told to gather. I'll be surrounded by people who love me as much

Martha Engber

as I love them. I'll eat, I'll laugh, I'll know life is imperfect, but I'll keep the journey going.

Finally, bliss is mine, baby.

252

Neptune's Daughter

she lifts from
the sea

brilliance rushing
from her head,

weighting eyelashes, dragging
hair down her back,

sucking blue shirt
to new skin,

her breasts small shells
of round, tight,

the cold all
she's known, till now,

her feet climbing
free, despite

waves that grab
for her elbows,

because her eyes
are already on the beyond

among the sandy hills
where a breeze

beats hearts
of rosehip while swaying

the wavy hairgrass
as birds roll

through a ribboning wind, crying
out until her face tilts up.

What she came from lunges for what
remains, her hips, her hands,

but they, too, come away
into the warm air,

an ephemeral softness
through which droplets

slip from wrists and sides, fingertips
and thighs.

All ascend toward the red of those rosehips,
the blue of that sky,

her pale ear angled to the bending
siren of birds

as she rises, finally seeing,
from the sea.

Acknowledgements

Writing this memoir was an emotionally rigorous task I could never have completed without the amazing support of dozens of people, an outcome that's furthered the lesson I've learned in writing this book: we are better humans when we connect with others.

I'd like to thank my beta readers who courageously faced the rawest version of this story: Melissa Slayton, Annalisa Crawford, Alan Tracey, Cathy Thrush and Paulette Boudreaux. Melissa gets an extra hug for so superbly guiding me through the final developmental edit.

No book could have been born, however, without Acquisitions Editor Melanie Faith's recommendation to publish the book. Once accepted, Publisher Jessica Bell and her intrepid literary partner, Publishing Director Amie McCracken, steered a straight course toward publication.

Considering my hope is for readers to better understand autism, neurodiversity and the diagnostic history of ASD, I'm grateful for discovering the many books and articles that have shed light in this area. These are the specific books I found invaluable: Liane Holliday Willey's *Pretending to be Normal: Living with Asperger's Syndrome*; Dr. Devon Price's *Unmasking Autism: Discovering the New Faces of Neurodiversity*; and Dr. Kristin Neff's *Self-Compassion: The Proven Power of Being Kind to Yourself.*

I'm also thankful to *The Aurorean* and *The Fictional Cafe* for first publishing several of the poems included in this book.

Lastly, there are no words adequate enough to express my profound thanks to my family—husband, son, daughter, sisters, brothers-in-law, nieces and nephews—for their support in telling my version of a story that's touched us all. I love you more than you know.

Vine Leaves Press

Enjoyed this book?
Go to *vineleavespress.com* to find more.
Subscribe to our newsletter: